D0560158

Sermon Outlines for Worship and Devotional Services

Compiled and Edited by
AL BRYANT, *Editor-in-Chief*
Christian Digest

ZONDERVAN PUBLISHING HOUSE
Grand Rapids, Michigan

TO YOU WHO USE THESE OUTLINES:

As the famous Dr. F. E. Marsh once said of a book of his own original sermon outlines, these outlines are "meant to be *suggestive to busy workers,* not crutches for lazy shirkers." That is also especially true of this compilation of "Looseleaf Sermon Outlines for Worship Services."

Gathered from many and varied sources, the 112 sermon outlines in this compilation are produced for the purpose of enriching *your* ministry to your people. Because every pastor is faced with the need for at least 52 different worship sermons and services each year, it was felt that this collection of outlines for sermons for worship services was the most urgently needed. More will follow: outlines for prayer meeting talks, evangelistic sermons, etc.

The pages are punched to fit the standard 3-ring looseleaf binder but may be punched by you to fit your own binder, should you already have one.

These outlines are dedicated to the ministry of not only comforting and challenging Christians, but also seeking lost souls for Christ. May they accomplish that purpose in *your* hands.

THE COMPILER

CONTENTS

Old Testament

WALKING WITH GOD

Enoch walked with God (Genesis 5:22).
We read of walking before, after and with God. In the first we have the thought of perfection (Genesis 17:11). In the second, obedience (Deuteronomy 13:4). But in the third of friendship and fellowship (Genesis 5:25).

I. GOD WANTS US TO WALK WITH HIM. I Corinthians 1:9
   A. John 1:3; Matthew 11:28. The yoke suggests two united.
II. CONDITIONS
   A. Acquaintance (Job 22:21).
   B. Agreement (Amos 3:3).
III. HOW ARE WE TO WALK?
   A. By Faith (II Corinthians 5:7).
   B. In the Light (I John 1:7).
   C. In the Newness of Life (Romans 6:4).
   D. In the Spirit (Galatians 5:16).
   E. In Love (Ephesians 5:1, 2).
   F. Circumspectly (Ephesians 5:15, 16).
   G. Worthily (Ephesians 4:1). —*Sermon Starters*
                                    P. E. HOLDCRAFT

WALKING WITH GOD

And Enoch walked with God (Genesis 5:22).
   I. IMPLIES FELLOWSHIP WITH GOD.
   II. IMPLIES SERVICE FOR GOD.
   III. IMPLIES PROGRESS IN HOLY LIVING.
   IV. BRINGS ASSURANCE OF SAFETY.
   V. GETS YOU SOMEWHERE.

                         —*Sermon Starters*
                         P. E. HOLDCRAFT

9

THE BURNING BUSH AN EMBLEM OF THE CHURCH

And the angel of the Lord appeared unto him in a flame of fire out of the midst of a bush: and he looked, and, behold, the bush burned with fire, and the bush was not consumed (Exodus 3:2).

I. THE TRUE CHURCH OF GOD IS NOT ASSOCIATED WITH EARTHLY GRANDEUR AND MAGNIFICENCE.

II. THE CONDITION OF THE CHURCH HAS EVER BEEN THAT OF TRIAL AND SUFFERING.

III. THE CHURCH OF GOD HAS WITHIN IT THE ELEMENT OF PERPETUITY. "NOT BURN"—NOT CONSUMED.

    (1) Look at this as a striking fact.

    (2) For this there is a sufficient reason—God was in the bush.

THEREFORE

1. Understand the nature of Christ's Church.
2. Abhor persecution.
3. Look to Jehovah for success.
4. Sympathize with the persecuted and the tried.

—The Tool Basket

WHAT HAVE YOU?

What is that in thine hand? (Exodus 4:2)

I. MOSES HAD A ROD, and it became a wand.

II. DAVID HAD A SLING, and used it to slay a giant.

III. A JEWISH MAID HAD A LITTLE VOICE, and used it to tell of the man of God (Naaman . . . Elisha).

IV. A LITTLE LAD HAD HIS LUNCH, and Jesus used it to feed a multitude.

V. A WIDOW HAD TWO MITES, but millions have been inspired by her giving.

VI. DORCAS HAD ONLY A SEWING KIT, but used it in a big way to help the poor.

"What is that in thine hand?"

—*Sermon Starters*
P. E. HOLDCRAFT

REMEMBER EGYPT!

. . . remember that thou wast a servant in the land of Egypt (Deuteronomy 5:15).

We are prone to remember the palaces and pleasures of Egypt. God admonishes us to remember its slavery. The memory of our former state should be:

I. AN ANTIDOTE TO DISCONTENT

Though the labors and trials of the wilderness are many, yet in Egypt we had more.

If we labor, it is not to make bricks without straw. If we are bereaved, at least we can bury our dead. Formerly our toil was for another, now it redounds to our own profit.

II. A STIMULUS TO ZEAL

Remembering Egypt, let us press on toward Canaan; let us give no advantage to our enemies. Knowing the terror of former slavery, fight manfully, that none may reduce us again to that condition.

III. A REASON FOR OBEDIENCE

Surely He who was so gracious as to deliver us has a right to our service.

If we made so many bricks for Pharoah, "What shall we render unto the Lord" If fear produced activity, how much more should love?

IV. WINGS FOR FAITH AND HOPE

Remember that God, who could deliver from Egypt, can and will bring to Canaan.

Surely He who has commenced our deliverance will complete it.

V. A CALL TO HUMILITY

I was but a servant, a slave. I owe all to my Deliverer. Without Him I were a slave again. "By grace I am what I am."

—Stems and Twigs

SAINTS IN GOD'S HAND

. . . all his saints are in thy hand (Deuteronomy 33:3).

I. WHO ARE SAINTS? They are children of God by regeneration. They are "Born of the Spirit," "Born again," "new creatures," "created in Christ Jesus unto good works."

II. SAINTS ARE IN GOD'S HAND. It may be said that all God's creatures are in His hand; but the saints are so in a peculiar sense. This will appear if we consider —

1. They are in His loving hand. His is the hand of a Father and surely He loves those whom He has made His children in so costly a manner, even through the incarnation and death of His own Son.

2. They are in His guiding hand. Well it is for them that they are not left to their own guidance. They know not the way in which they should go. They know not what is best for them.

3. They are in His protecting hand. How greatly they

need protection! They need protection from themselves, protection from the evil influences of the world, and from the snares of Satan. His hand is stretched forth for their defence.

4. They are in His chastening hand. He chastens them with the paternal reluctance exemplified in a wise earthly father (Lamentations 3:33). His love prompts the application of the chastening rod (Hebrews 12:5-11).

5. They are in His sustaining hand. He holds them up otherwise they would sink beneath the waves of sorrow. The hour of death comes apace. How greatly will they need divine suport in that hour when all human helpers fail!

—Notes of Sermons

SEVEN-FOLD PRIVILEGE OF THE CHILD OF GOD

SAVED — — — —	Deuteronomy 33:29
SECURED — — —	Deuteronomy 33:3
SEPARATED — — —	Deuteronomy 33:16
SATISFIED — — —	Deuteronomy 33:23
SHELTERED — — —	Deuteronomy 33:29
SEATED — — — —	Deuteronomy 33:3
SACRIFICING — — —	Deuteronomy 33:19

—Pegs for Preachers

THE HAPPY PEOPLE

The eternal God is thy refuge, and underneath are the everlasting arms; and he shall thrust out the enemy from before thee; and shall say, Destroy them . . . (Deuteronomy 33: 27-29).

I. THE PEOPLE DESCRIBED
   A. A saved people

    B. A happy people
    C. A victorious people
II. The Nature of Their Blessedness
    A. Their shelter
    B. Their support
    C. Their security
    D. Their provisions
    E. Their defence
    F. Their assurance of victory

—Pulpit Germs

THE EVERLASTING ARMS

. . . underneath are the everlasting arms . . . (Deuteronomy 33:27).

  I. The Arms of Everlasting Power (Jeremiah 31:17; 27:5; Luke 1:51)

 II. The Arms of Everlasting Salvation (Isaiah 45:17; 52:10; John 10:28; I Peter 1:5)

III. The Arms of Everlasting Redemption (Psalm 77:15; Exodus 6:6; Acts 13:17)

IV. The Arms of Everlasting Protection (Exodus 15:16; Psalm 34:7; 91:16; John 10:28, 29)

 V. The Arms of Everlasting Sovereignty (Ezekiel 20:33; Isaiah 40:10; Psalm 97:1; 99:1; Revelation 19:6)

VI. The Arms of Everlasting Judgment (Isaiah 51:5; Jeremiah 21:5; John 5:22)

VII. The Arms of Everlasting Victory (Psalm 98:1; I Corinthians 15:57; I John 5:4)

—Treasures of Bible Truth
William H. Schweinfurth

HOW TO "BE STRONG"

As Illustrated in the Exhortation to Joshua (Chapter 1)

I. GOD'S PROMISE to rest on—"Be strong, for thou shalt cause this people to inherit" (verse 6)

II. GOD'S PRECEPTS to rejoice in—"Be strong and very courageous, that thou mayest observe to do" (verse 7)

III. GOD'S PRESENCE to realize daily—"Be strong and of good courage, for the Lord thy God is with thee" (verse 9)

IV. GOD'S PEOPLE to be responsible for—"Only be strong and of a good courage" (verse 18)

—*Twelve Baskets Full*

A GREAT GOD

II Chronicles 16:9

I. HE SEES — "The eyes of the Lord."

II. HE ACTS — "run to and fro."

III. HE IS INTERESTED — "throughout the whole earth."

IV. HE MANIFESTS HIMSELF — "to show himself strong."

V. HE HELPS — "in behalf of them."

VI. HE ENCOURAGES — "Whose heart is perfect toward him."

—*Snappy Sermon Starters*

LOYALTY TO GOD'S HOUSE

We will not forsake the house of our God (Nehemiah 10:39).

I. BECAUSE IT IS THE PLACE WHERE GOD DWELLS.

II. BECAUSE IT IS THE PLACE WHERE HE REVEALS HIMSELF.

III. BECAUSE IT IS THE PLACE WHERE HE TEACHES.

IV. BECAUSE IT IS THE PLACE WHERE HE CONVERTS.

V. BECAUSE IT IS THE PLACE WHERE HE SANCTIFIES.

VI. BECAUSE IT IS THE PLACE WHERE HE HEARS PRAYER.
VII. BECAUSE IT IS THE PLACE WHERE HE PREPARES THE
    SAINTS FOR HEAVEN.

—Snappy Sermon Starters

PRECIOUS TRIALS

. . . when he hath tried me, I shall come forth as gold
(Job 23:10).

I. TRIAL IS A DIVINE PROCESS
    A. God's will appoints them
    B. God's love effects them
    C. God's presence comforts in them
II. TRIAL IS A USEFUL PROCESS
    A. It is a token of value
    B. It is a test of genuineness
    C. It is a medium of purification
    D. It is a preparation for service

—Pulpit Germs

THE HAPPY AND THE UNHAPPY MAN

Psalm 1:1-6

Two characters are brought before us; the one is pro-
nounced happy, and the other miserable. Three things are
said to characterize *the good man*:—

I. HE SHUNS EVIL COMPANIONS
    A. Here is a classification of the wicked; ungodly,
    sinners, scornful; that is, without God — opposed
    to God — and having contempt for God.
    B. Here is a graduated scale of depravity — walking,
    standing, sitting.

II. HE DELIGHTS IN THE WORD OF GOD.
    A. The word "law" here stands for the whole of divine revelation.
        1. Show me a holy, God-fearing man, and I will show you one who loves the Bible.
        2. And what a man loves he thinks about; and so we read, "In his law he meditates day and night."

III. HE IS LIKE A TREE PLANTED.
    A. He is like a tree in his growth.
        1. "Consider the lilies, *how* they grow."
    B. "A tree planted" — that is, a tree cared for.
        1. Such a tree is fenced in to protect it from wild beasts.
        2. It is staked to preserve it from the wind.
        3. It is watered in the time of drouth.

Three things are affirmed of *the wicked man*:—

I. HE WILL BE CONDEMNED IN THE JUDGMENT.
    A. "Shall not stand in the Judgment."
        1. This does not mean that he will not be present; "for we shall all appear before the Judgment Seat of Christ;" but the word "stand" here is a law term, and means the same as to be "justified."

II. HIS COMPANIONSHIP WITH THE RIGHTEOUS WILL TERMINATE.
    A. "Nor sinners in the congregation of the righteous." Farewell, holy Sabbaths; farewell, house of God; farewell, praying father and mother!

III. HIS END WILL BE DESTRUCTION:—
    A. "The way of the ungodly shall perish."
    B. How much that means we do not know, but it is a doom that Jesus wept over, and died to save us from.

—Revival Sermons in Outline

THE MOUTH

THE MOUTH BY NATURE

1. Full of cursing and deceit ...... Psalm 10:7
2. Speaking proudly .... Psalm 17:10
3. Given to evil .... Psalm 50:19
4. Speaking vanity .... Psalm 144:8
5. Covered with violence .... Proverbs 10:6
6. Pouring out foolishness .... Proverbs 15:2
7. Ends in destruction .... Proverbs 18:7

THE MOUTH BY GRACE

1. Crying unto the Lord .... Psalm 66:17
2. Filled with His Praise .... Psalm 71:8
3. Showing His righteousness ...... Psalm 71:15
4. Filled with laughter .... Psalm 126:2
5. A well of life .... Proverbs 10:11
6. Satisfied .... Proverbs 18:20
7. Confessing the Lord Jesus .... Romans 10:9

—Twelve Baskets Full

REJOICING IN SALVATION

. . . my heart shall rejoice in thy salvation (Psalm 13:5).

I. SALVATION IS OF THE LORD

The salvation in which David rejoiced was not that of:
   A. Philosophy
   B. Education
   C. Morality
   D. Good works
   E. The church
but *Thy* (God's) salvation

II. THE CHARACTERISTICS OF THE LORD'S SALVATION
   A. It is universal. (John 3:16; I Timothy 2:6)
   B. It is free. (Isaiah 55:1; Revelation 22:17)

C. It is perfect. It meets all the wants of sinful men. Knowledge for the ignorant, pardon for the guilty, etc.

D. It is present. (II Corinthians 6:2; Hebrews 3:7)

E. It is eternal.

III. The Joy of This Salvation

A. It brings peace and joy into the soul.

B. It brings us into a conscious union with God.

C. It inspires with the hope of glory.

—100 *Sermon Outlines*

THE SHEPHERD PSALM — A Study

The Lord Jesus is Spoken of in Psalm 23 As:

1. The Shepherd .... (verse 1)
2. The Leader .... (verse 2)
3. The Restorer .... (verse 3)
4. The Comforter .... (verse 4)
5. The Preparer .... (verse 5)
6. The Anointer .... (verse 5)
7. The Follower .... (verse 6)

—*Twelve Baskets Full*

DIVISION OF PSALM 23

1. The Lord is *my* Shepherd .... Possession
2. I shall *not want* .... Provision
3. He maketh me to *lie down* in green pastures .... Position
4. He leadeth me beside *still* *waters* .... Pasturage

5. He restoreth *my soul* ....Personal
6. He *leadeth* me in the paths of
   righteousness ....Progress
7. For *His name's* sake ....Purpose
8. Yea, though I walk through the
   valley of the shadow of death ....Parting
9. I will *fear no evil* ....Peace
10. For *Thou art with me* ....Protection
11. Thy *rod* and Thy *staff* they com-
    fort me ....Pilgrimage
12. Thou *preparest* a table for me ....Participation
13. In the *presence* of my enemies ......Presence
14. Thou anointest my head with oil ....Preparation
15. My cup *runneth over* ....Plenty
16. *Surely* goodness and mercy shall
    follow me all the days of my life....Persuasion
17. And I will *dwell* in the house of
    the Lord forever ....Place

—Twelve Baskets Full

PSALM 23

PERFECT SATISFACTION......................"Shall not want"
PERFECT REST ...."Lying down"
PERFECT PEACE ...."Waters of quietness"
PERFECT WALK ...."Paths of righteousness"
PERFECT CONFIDENCE ...."Will fear no evil"
PERFECT POWER ...."Anointest my head"
PERFECT JOY ...."My cup runneth over"

—Pegs for Preachers

GOD'S WAY

Shew me thy ways, O Lord; teach me thy paths (Psalm 25:4).

I. ITS CHARACTERISTICS

A way of truth (Psalm 25:5)
A way of mercy (Psalm 25:10)
A way of obedience (Psalm 69:32)
A way of peace (Proverbs 3:17)
A way of holiness (Isaiah 35:8)
A way of safety (Isaiah 35:9)
A way of prosperity (Genesis 24:56)

II. NATURAL MAN IGNORANT—MUST BE TAUGHT.

"Teach me" (Psalm 27:11)
"Show me" (Psalm 25:4)
"Lead me" (Psalm 25:5)

III. WHO MAY KNOW GOD'S WAY?

The meek (I Peter 5:5)
The obedient (John 7:17)
The man of faith (Acts 3:16; John 3:16)

IV. HOW MAY HE LEARN?

Through Christ (John 6:40; John 8:12; John 10:28; John 10:9)

—*Sermons in a Nutshell*

LOVE FOR THE HOUSE OF GOD

Lord, I have loved the habitation of Thine house, and the place where Thine honour dwelleth (Psalm 26:8).

I. GOD'S HOUSE IN ITS RELATION TO THE DEVOUT WORSHIPER

A. As the appointed place for Divine worship.

We are not indifferent to the truth that there is no spot on earth where the throne of grace is not accessible. Yet the sacred sanctuary, set apart for

God's special worship, and hallowed by the prayers
of many of His people, claims to be regarded with
special love and reverence, whether it be tabernacle or temple, church or chapel.

B. As the place where God has especially promised to
reveal Himself to His people.

God allowed a visible emblem of His Presence to
dwell in the Tabernacle of old; and in His House,
today. He is especially present to convict, to comfort, and to bless.

C. God's House is loved by the Christian because of
hallowed experience there.

Its services develop and sanctify the social bond
in all its relations. It is loved as the type of the
house not made with hands, eternal in the heavens.

II. SOME OF THE TOKENS OF TRUE REGARD AND LOVE FOR
GOD'S HOUSE

A. A desire to attend it.

B. A willingness to support it, both by taking part in
its services, and by loyally and generously giving
of our substance for its maintenance.

C. By consistency of life, lest outsiders be given cause
of offence against religion, because of the sad dif-
ference between the prayers and practices of
Christians.

—*Sermons in a Nutshell*

A CALL TO WORSHIP

*O magnify the Lord with me, and let us exalt his name to-
gether* (Psalm 34:3).

This text is a clear call to sincere worship. To respond
to the call will enable souls to have strength to meet the
difficulties of life. Among the lessons in the text are:

I. THE PURPOSE OF WORSHIP IS STATED

"O magnify the Lord." The primary purpose of worship is to magnify the Lord, and to exalt His holy name that we may receive strength in so doing. The Lord is worthy of worship. His character is good, His deeds are merciful, His acts are just, and His love is everlasting. Reverence the Lord! Adore Him! Magnify His Works! Exalt His Holy Name!

II. THE PEOPLE FOR WORSHIP ARE MENTIONED

"With me." The psalmist expresses his praise to the Father and then calls for all people everywhere to join him in holy worship. Truly all people should worship the Lord for His goodness. In other places in the Psalms the writer calls on all things to praise the Lord, even the heavens to be glad, the earth to rejoice, the fields to be happy, and the trees to sing for joy. Surely all men should praise and worship God. All men need to worship Him. All would be blessed in worship.

III. THE PLACE OF WORSHIP IS INTIMATED

"Let us exalt his name together." This calls for the unity of an assembly. It calls for people to assemble themselves together and worship the Lord in the unity of purpose. It is a glorious truth that men may worship the Lord in any and all places. But it is true also that there is an inspiration in a congregation worshiping the Lord together in the beauty of holiness. It is glorious that the people of our nation are within easy reach of a place erected and dedicated unto the Lord for worship.

IV. THE PLAN OF WORSHIP IS SUGGESTED

"His praise shall continually be in my mouth." Man may praise the Lord in song, and prayer, and testimony and witnessing. These methods may be used in private and in public as men seek to worship and

magnify the Lord and His blessed Name and work.
"O magnify the Lord." Worship His Holy Name!

FOUR P's IN PSALM FORTY-TWO

I.	DAVID PANTING	— — —	Psalm 42:1
II.	DAVID POURING	— — —	Psalm 42:4
III.	DAVID POUTING	— — —	Psalm 42:5
IV.	DAVID PRAISING	— — —	Psalm 42:11

—Twelve Baskets Full

TOGETHER

We took sweet counsel together and walked to the house of God in company (Psalm 55:14).

Together-ness (co-operation) should characterize:

I. OUR WORSHIP.

Private worship and radio worship have their value but no substitute for public worship.

"Forsake not the assembling of yourselves together."

II. OUR FINANCIAL SUPPORT OF THE CHURCH.

"On the first day of the week let every one of you lay by . . ." (I Corinthians 16:2).

III. OUR WARFARE FOR CHRIST.

Christian soldiers must not be divided, or scattered.

"So make we all one company,
    Love's golden cord the tether;
And come what may, we'll climb the way,
    Together, ah! together."

—Snappy Sermon Starters

FOLLOW YOUR LEADER

And he led them on safely, so that they feared not (Psalm 78:53).

I. LED.
II. LED ON.
III. LED ON SAFELY.
Hence they feared not.
IV. WHO IS OUR LEADER?
"I have given him for a leader" (Isaiah 55:4).
V. WHOM DOES HE LEAD?
A. The redeemed (Exodus 15:13).
B. Those who know His mercy (Isaiah 49:10).
VI. HOW DOES HE LEAD?
A. In the way we should go (Isaiah 48:17).
B. "In the paths of righteousness" (Psalm 23:3).
Hence there is no need to fear (see Isaiah 41:10-13; Psalm 23:4; Hebrews 13:5, 6).

—*Snappy Sermon Starters*

THE CHURCH COMPARED TO A VINE

Return, we beseech thee, O God of hosts: look down from heaven, and behold and visit this vine (Psalm 80:14).

The ancient church which the Almighty brought out of Egypt, is here compared to a vine. Christ, the great Teacher, used a like figure when He said, "I am the vine, and ye are the branches." Let us consider some of the particulars in which the church may be said to be like a vine:

I. THE ROOT OF THE VINE.
A. The root of the vine is Christ.
1. Not beautiful in appearance, but an unsightly object.
2. When men saw Christ, they said, "There is

no form, nor comeliness in him that we should desire him."

3. When He is spoken of as a stone, He is said to be "a stone disallowed of the builders," but —

II. THE WEAKNESS OF THE VINE.

A. It is a clinging plant.

B. It cannot stand alone.

C. It cannot support itself.

III. THE VINE, THOUGH A FRAIL PLANT, GROWS RAPIDLY.

A. How weak a plant Christianity appeared at the first, but how rapidly it spread!

1. Peter planted it among the Gentiles when he preached to Cornelius and his family.

2. Philip, the evangelist, carried it to Samaria.

3. Next it took root in the Syrian Antioch.

4. Paul planted this precious vine all along the shores of the Mediterranean, and in the towns and cities of Asia Minor.

IV. IT IS THE FRUIT OF THE VINE THAT MAKES IT OF VALUE.

A. It is for this, and this alone, that men cultivate it.

1. Christ says to His church, to His people, "In this is your Father glorified that ye bear much fruit."

2. And again He says, "My Father is the husbandman . . . and every branch that beareth fruit, he purgeth it that it may bear more fruit."

V. THE VINE REQUIRES PRUNING.

A. Fruitless branches must be cut off.

B. This is actually necessary; the vine must be pruned if it is to be fruitful.

1. But bear in mind that this requires great wisdom and prudence. A man with a sharp

knife might soon spoil and ruin a splendid vine.

VI. THE VINE GROWS ON, AND BEAUTIFIES AND ADORNS ROCKY AND UNSIGHTLY PLACES, such as:
  A. The sides of old buildings.
  B. The rocky and barren sides of hills and mountains.
  C. Vineyards were the beauty of Palestine.

VII. THAT LAND IS ALMOST A DESERT TODAY.
  A. Its hillsides are rocky and bare.
  B. The terraces have been broken down.
  C. Where the vines once flourished, desolation now reigns.

VIII. SO, TOO, THIS VINE BEAUTIFIES AND ADORNS THE EARTH.
  A. Wherever it has been planted and carefully cultivated, there is spiritual beauty.
  B. Wherever it has been allowed to die, there desolation and ruin reign.
    1. How must the thoughtful traveler feel depressed, as he surveys the barren and desolate appearance of Palestine, and remembers that where nothing now exists but naked rocks, vineyards once flourished.
    2. And what must be the feelings of the thoughtful Christian who visits those lands where the Gospel once flourished, but where it was allowed to die, and where pagan darkness now reigns!

IX. THE VINE CAN BE PROPAGATED IN TWO WAYS.
  A. From the seed.
  B. From cuttings or branches.

X. SO, TOO, THE GOSPEL CHURCHES ARE PROPAGATED, AND CHRISTIANITY EXTENDED IN TWO WAYS.

A. By the seed of the kingdom, which is the Word of God.
B. By branches of the vine, that is, by believers themselves.
C. There are various ways in which the good seed can be sown—by tracts, by Bibles, etc.
    1. To propagate the vine by cuttings seems a severe way, but it is one that God has often used.
    2. When the storms of persecution fell on the first church in Jerusalem, "They that were scattered abroad went everywhere preaching the word," and so the vine spread and took root in new places.

—Revival Sermons in Outlines

THE ETERNAL CITY

Glorious things are spoken of thee, O city of God (Psalm 87:3).

I. A PLACE OF SUPREME HAPPINESS.
"Fulness of Joy" (Psalm 16:11).
"God shall wipe away all tears" (Revelation 7:17).

II. A PLACE OF SURPASSING BEAUTY.
"Eye hath not seen nor ear heard" (I Corinthians 2:9).
"The half has never been told"

III. A PLACE OF REVELATION.
"Now we know in part, then . . ." (I Corinthians 13:12).

IV. A PLACE OF FREEDOM FROM PAIN.
"There shall be no more pain" (Revelation 21:4).
Deaf . . . Blind . . . Lame . . . Healed (Isaiah 35).

V. A PLACE OF REUNION.
"Then . . . face to face" (I Corinthians 13:12).

"Many shall come from the east and west . . ."
(Matthew 8:11).

—*Snappy Sermon Starters*

THE PURPOSE OF PRAISE

Bless the Lord, O my soul, and forget not all his benefits
(Psalm 103:2).

I. IT IS PRAISE TO GOD

"Bless the Lord." The Lord gives life and sustains
it. We live and move and have our life in Him. We
should praise Him for every good and perfect gift.
We should praise Him for all physical and spiritual
blessings. The Lord is worthy of all praise from all
the people in all the earth.

II. IT IS PRAISE FROM THE SOUL

"O my soul." The praise uttered here comes from
a full heart. It is the very expression of the soul.
The praise expressed here is from all the faculties
and powers of the being. It expresses all that can
come from the intellect, the feeling and the will of a
grateful personality. This praise is the voice of the
sincere soul. Such praise will lift the soul into the
very presence of God.

III. IT IS PRAISE FOR BENEFITS

"Forget not all his benefits." Praise the Lord for
all He does for us in the physical and the spiritual
realms. Study the seven benefits of the Lord mentioned in Psalm 103:3-6. He forgives our sins and
saves our souls and we become children of His. He
is the Great Physician and can heal all the diseases
of the body when it is in accord with his Holy will.
He preserves life, crowns with loving-kindness, sup-
plies every good thing that life needs, and gives con-

tinually the strength we need. How gracious is the
Lord! What benefits to have Him always! Praise
Him! Bless His name!

—*Sermons in Outline*
JEROME O. WILLIAMS

THE WORD OF GOD

*Thy word have I hid in mine heart, that I might not sin
against thee* (Psalm 119:11).

I.	LIVES	—	—	—	—	I Peter 1:23
II.	ABIDES	—	—	—	—	I John 2:14
III.	PIERCES		—	—	—	Hebrews 4:12
IV.	SANCTIFIES		—	—	—	I Timothy 4:4, 5
V.	DISCERNS		—	—	—	Hebrews 4:12
VI.	WORKS	—	—	—	—	I Thessalonians 2:13
VII.	PREVAILS		—	—	—	Acts 19:20

—*Treasures of Bible Truth*

THE MERCHANT

*The merchandise of it is better than the merchandise of
silver, and the gain thereof than fine gold* (Proverbs 3:14).

This is one of the most forceful and impressive of all
the proverbs of Solomon. He takes a merchant who traffics
in silver and gold to set forth the reality and activities
of religion. The holy experience of grace and Christ's
righteousness in the soul is as much of a reality as silver
and gold is real.

I. THE ANALOGY.

    A. The merchant wisely locates his business for suc-
cess.

        1. So the Christian will first locate his gifts of

prayer, song, strength, and whatever God has given him for service.

B. The wise merchant fills his place with goods for sale.

    1. The Christian for happiness and usefulness will see to it that his heart is filled with holy experience, grace and truth.

C. The successful merchant advertises his business to the world.

    1. The Christian will likewise ever be ready to give his testimony to win souls.

D. The merchant has great concern about the prices of goods and general state of the market.

    1. The child of God will in like manner have deep interest about the affairs and state of Zion.

E. The retail merchant keeps up a frequent correspondence with the great trading marts.

    1. So with the faithful Christian.

    2. He will be constant in prayer, and have correspondence with the divine Lord.

F. Merchants differ in talents, some with large and some with smaller gifts.

    1. So with Christians; but all are to give service to the best of their ability.

G. The successful merchant accommodates himself to his customers.

    1. The faithful Christian will always be on the alert to suit his words, acts, and influence to the best good of those around him.

H. A good merchant both dispenses and receives benefits.

    1. He sells for the benefit of others, and receives profits himself.

    2. So the useful Christian — he gives blessings to

others and thereby receives benefit to his own soul.

I. The successful merchant closes up his life work with large gain.

    1. How many earnest and faithful Christians will have their crowns bedecked with stars, and yet walk the golden streets with those they have led to Christ.

II. THE APPLICATION.

Will every one who hears this discourse enter at once into holy traffic for Jesus as you never have before?

—Revival Sermons in Outline

KEEPING COMPANY WITH FOOLS

But a companion of fools shall be destroyed (Proverbs 13:20).

I. WHO ARE FOOLS?

    A. Those who occupy their time and thought with trifles.

    B. Those who "make a mock at sin."

    C. Those who neglect important truths and realities.

    D. Those who do not prepare for great and unavoidable events.

II. HOW DO WE WALK WITH THEM?

    A. By frequenting their company.

    B. By following their example.

    C. By reading their books.

III. WHAT WILL BE THE CONSEQUENCES?

    A. We shall be tainted with their vices.

    B. We shall share their present sufferings.

    C. We shall be involved in their eternal doom.

—Snappy Sermon Starters
W. W. WYTHE

SOUL-WINNING

He that winneth souls is wise (Proverbs 11:30).

Our Prayer—Acts 6:6
Our Field—Mark 5:19, 20
Our Time—Matthew 21:28
Our Motive—II Corinthians 5:14
Our Helper—John 15:5
Our Theme—John 3:16
Our Message—Romans 1:16
Our Power—John 16:7, 11
Our Example—Luke 2:49
Our Reward—II Timothy 4:8

TRAINING THE CHILD

Train up a child in the way he should go: and when he is old, he will not depart from it (Proverbs 22:6).

This text is a vital message to parents. Hear it. We call attention to three things in the text:

I. The Reason for Training.
  A. "Train up a child."
    1. The child is helpless.
    2. He is needy.
    3. He is wholly dependent.
  B. Train the child because he is the heir of the past, the happiness of the present, and the hope of the future.
  C. Your child is your opportunity and responsibility from the Lord.
II. The Rule for Training.
  A. A. "In the way he should go."
    1. The training of the child should be upward.
    2. The child should be led to salvation of the soul, to service of the life, and to safety for eternity.

III. THE RESULTS OF TRAINING.
    A. "When he is old, he will not depart from it."
        1. The course of life is fixed in early days.
        2. The goal to be gained is given in youth.
        3. Abiding habits of life are fixed while children
           are young.
    B. If the right course is fixed, if the ideal goal is
       given, and if righteous habits are formed in child-
       hood, the same will be pursued in the years to
       come.   —*Sermons in Outlines*

OUR WONDERFUL SAVIOUR

. . . his name shall be called Wonderful . . . (Isaiah 9:6)

W—WONDERFUL IN HIS WORK —	—(John 7:21; 9:4; 17:4)
O—WONDERFUL IN HIS OFFERING	—(Heb. 10:10, 14, 18)
N—WONDERFUL IN HIS NATURE	—(Col. 2:9; John 10: 30; 14:9)
D—WONDERFUL IN HIS DEEDS —	—(John 5:19; Mark 7:37)
E—WONDERFUL IN HIS EXAMPLE	—(I Peter 2:21)
R—WONDERFUL IN HIS REDEMPTION	(Col. 1:14; Eph. 1:7; I Peter 1:18-20)
F—WONDERFUL IN HIS FORBEARANCE	(Mark 15:3-5)
U—WONDERFUL IN HIS UNION —	—(John 17:21, 22, 23)
L—WONDERFUL IN HIS LOVE —	—(John 15:13; 13:1)

—*Treasures of Bible Truth*

THE BEST PROTECTION

Thou wilt keep him in perfect peace, whose mind is stayed on thee: because he trusteth in thee (Isaiah 26:3).

  I. THE RECIPIENT OF THE PROMISE—The man "whose mind is stayed."

"Mind," in margin "thought," includes imagination, idea, desire, whole heart. "Stayed"; by deliberate act of faith shifting all care, responsibility, result, to the One best able to take it; and being, in consequence, left at peace from all worry.

II. THE PRECIOUS ASSURANCE HERE GIVEN—"Thou wilt keep him in perfect peace."

Peace is longed for by all: individuals and nations. It is God's gift, bestowed only on those who fulfill His conditions.

Peace, God-given, is peace at its fullest. "Perfect peace," in the original "Peace, peace," language failing to express its fulness — like ff or pp in music, for much loudness or much softness.

III. THE SIMPLE, YET AMPLE REASON ASSIGNED—"Because he trusteth in Thee."

It is the direct outcome of faith. So simple that none can fail to find it. "He trusteth in Thee"; ample ground for faith, for Jehovah is the Covenant God.

The "trust" of the Old Testament is just the "faith" of the New. Let us, therefore, who have come to God through Christ, allow the peace of God to rule in our hearts. So shall we have peace indeed in our hearts and homes—peace in the present, and peace for the future.

—*Sermons in a Nutshell*

WITH WINGS AS EAGLES

They that wait upon the Lord shall renew their strength; they shall mount up with wings as eagles (Isaiah 40:31).

Many metaphors and similes are used in Scripture to help the people of God to understand themselves: sheep, salt, light, branches, soldiers, leaven, etc.

In the text the man of God is compared to the greatest of the fowls of the air, the eagle.

I. THE EAGLE IS NOTED FOR GREAT STRENGTH.
   A. Christians should be "strong in the Lord" etc.
   B. Christians should never be "weary in well-doing."

II. THE EAGLE IS NOTED FOR ITS FARSIGHTEDNESS.
   A. "The Christian on his knees sees more than the philosopher on tiptoes."
   B. Stephen's "eagle eyes"—vision of Son of God.
   C. Daniel's window open toward Jerusalem.

III. THE EAGLE RISES ABOVE THE WORLD, WHICH IS ENVELOPED BY GASES, SMOKE, DUST AND CLOUDS.
   A. The Christian rises above the sordid things of the world.
   B. The Christian walks on the earth, but his head is above the clouds.
   C. Man's soul longs for freedom from sin.

IV. THE EAGLE IS NOTED FOR LONGEVITY.
   A. The Christian will live forever.

—*Snappy Sermon Starters*
PAUL E. HOLDCRAFT

THE ANTIDOTE TO FEAR

Fear thou not; for I am with thee . . ." (Isaiah 41:10).

Fear is common to man, increased by, if it does not originate in a consciousness of sin. The text indicates three reasons why the Christian should not be afraid.

I. GOD'S PRESENCE
   "I am with thee"
   Powerful, wise; loving

II. GOD'S RELATIONSHIP
   "I am *thy* God"
   These words imply on our part reverence, obedience

and submission; on His part guardianship and blessing. We naturally take special care of that which is our own.

III. God's Promise

A. "I will strengthen thee"—fortify thy heart against trial and suffering.

B. "I will help thee"—render thee personal assistance; direct, protect, fight with and for thee.

C. "I will uphold thee"
"The right hand of My righteousness" My faithful right hand: i.e. a hand that could be relied upon.
The right hand is generally used for work.
The right hand is offered in friendship.
The right hand is placed on those whom we wish to honor.

—The Preacher's Treasury

WITNESSES

Ye are my witnesses (Isaiah 43:10).

I. Why Has God Chosen a Believer for This Work?

A. Because he knows experimentally more of God than any other being. Angels could witness of His majesty and goodness. Devils, of His wrath and justice. All men, of His wisdom. But a child of God, while witnessing to all these, can tell of His mercy, of His forgiving love, of His forbearance, tenderness, and loving-kindness.

B. Because he can have no greater joy. The bride's delight is to point out her Lord, saying, "This is my friend; this is my beloved." It is by grace we are permitted to testify of Christ.

C. Because of our being constantly in the presence of our fellow-men. He would have the world without excuse. For from her very midst He raises up His witnesses.

II. THE THINGS A BELIEVER MUST POSSESS IN ORDER TO WITNESS FOR CHRIST.

    A. *Knowledge.* He must know by experience of the truth of God's Word. His life must be one "amen" to the words of his Lord. Thus, the Master says, "My yoke is easy," "Him that cometh" — the witness says, It is so; His yoke is easy; He has received and saved *me*.

    B. *Veracity.* However distasteful to men, we must speak the truth. The martyrs died amid flames because they would speak the truth as they themselves apprehended it.

    C. *Consistency.* Can one who says "this" today and "that" tomorrow, be believed? If you are most sanctimonious on Sunday and most worldly all the week, who will value your testimony?

    D. *Patience.* In our courts of law a witness has often long waiting. And though he attests the uprightness of a beggar, he waits. Remember, we witness of the Judge!

    E. *Boldness, firmness.* The world will do its cross-examining trying to catch us in our speech, as it did Christ.

III. THE BEST METHODS CHRIST'S WITNESS CAN ADOPT.

What are they? A parade of private devotion? Learned expositions of your creed? Denunciation of your opponents? Seclusion in a hermit's cell? No, but rather —

    A. A daily manifestation of heart-loyalty to Christ.

    B. A daily feeding on His promises, thus showing contentment and hope.

    C. A growing in His likeness.

    D. The display of the graces of His Spirit.

—Stems & Twigs

THE DESIRE OF ALL NATIONS

And the desire of all nations shall come: and I will fill this house with glory, saith the Lord of Hosts (Haggai 2:7).

I. JESUS WAS THE DESIRE OF ALL NATIONS:
   A. As the Kinsman of the whole family.
   B. Because He only could bestow those precious blessings which the world needed.
   C. Because all nations shall one day be made happy in Him.

II. HE APPEARED:
   A. At the very period marked out for His birth.
   B. In the very manner which had been foretold.
   C. For the performance of the very work which had been before marked out for Him.

III. THE PROPHET HAGGAI MENTIONS CERTAIN REMARKABLE EVENTS WHICH SHOULD DISTINGUISH THE MESSIAH'S COMING:
   A. All nations were to be shaken.
   B. The Jewish Temple should be filled with His glory.
                              —*Snappy Sermon Starters*

New Testament

THE NAME OF JESUS

Thou shalt call His name Jesus, for He shall save His people from their sins (Matthew 1:21).

Almost every historic person in the Bible bears an appropriate name; thus the name came to be identified with the person. In this text the name Jesus is declared to be descriptive of the person and the work of Christ.

I. LET ME CALL YOUR ATTENTION TO THE SAVIOUR.
   Jesus signifies: "Jehovah that saves." So Jesus is

Divine: He saves His people from their sins. Not the word, not the ordinances, but Jesus Himself.

II. LOOK AT THE SALVATION.

    A. Jesus saves from sin by bestowing forgiveness — full forgiveness, free, immediate and irreversible.

    B. Jesus saves His people from the pollution of sin; not in their sins, but from their sins. It is true that holiness is progressive, but the Christian cannot and does not love sin. Nor can he live in sin as the choice and habit of his life. This salvation shall be completed in heaven.

III. LET US LOOK AT THE SAVED.

"He shall save His people."

    A. Who are His people?

They must have been at one time in their sins. Therefore no one need despair.

"But does not the phrase speak of election? And how do I know that I am elected?"

Your business is not with election but with your calling, and you may make you calling sure by believing. Whosoever believeth in Him shall not perish. "Whosoever." Every one feels that includes him. "Whosoever believeth." Does that include you?

               —Three Hundred Outlines on the New Testament

THE CHRISTIAN'S LIGHT

Let your light so shine before men, that they may see your good works, and glorify your Father which is in heaven (Matthew 5:16).

Christ, the Light of the world, says to His followers, "Ye are the light of the world." There is no real discrepancy between the two statements: the city is lit by lamps and yet it is the electricity that does it all.

I. There Is First the Positive Injunction that Christians Are to Do Everything in Their Power to Secure that Their Light Shall Shine As Brightly As Possible.

This is to be done:—

A. By the position we take up.
   1. A lamp on the floor will not send out its rays so widely as if it were suspended from the ceiling.
   2. The Christian should connect himself with the Church, let his light shine by joining the company of those who confess with their mouths the Lord Jesus.

B. By the character which we form.
   1. Character is the most important thing in the world.
   2. There is no eloquence so powerful as a good man's life.

C. By the exertions we make for the conversion of fellow men.
   1. By these we benefit ourselves; let a man tie up his hand so that it becomes motionless, and by and by it will become withered and powerless like the limb of an Indian devotee.

II. Look at the Negative Side of this Injunction.

A. We should remove everything that tends either to obscure or to hide our light, or which so affects it as to make it suggestive of ourselves rather than of God.
   1. We should get rid of the undue reserve by which multitudes are characterized.
   2. We must keep ourselves clear from all practical inconsistencies.
   3. We should avoid all self display. The best style in writing is that which gives the thought with

such transparency that the reader sees nothing
else; and that is the noblest Christian character
which shows the most of Christ.

—Three Hundred Outlines on the New Testament

THE DUTY OF DISCIPLES

Seek ye first the kingdom of God, and his righteousness
(Matthew 6:33).

It should be the supreme purpose of everyone to seek
the kingdom of God. We study the text through five questions.

I. WHAT IS TO BE DONE?

"Seek." Put your heart into this enterprise. Seek
earrnestly, diligently, enthusiastically, steadily, with
your whole life, hands, head and heart.

II. WHO IS TO SEEK?

"Ye." All who believe in the Lord Jesus Christ. All
who name the Name of Christ. All who are members
of His Church and all who have a desire to do His
way and will. All who have had an experience of
grace and possess a new heart, a new purpose, a new
hope, a new outlook, and a new Master. "Seek ye."

III. WHEN SHALL WE SEEK?

"First." In time. In aim. In activity.

IV. WHAT SHALL WE SEEK?

His kingdom, and His righteousness. Seek to be right
in every relation of life, in relation to God, to Christ,
to the Church, to all Christians, to all sinners.

V. WHY SHOULD WE SEEK?

Because when we attain righteousness and seek the
kingdom, all lesser blessings will be added unto us.
When we seek the kingdom and righteousness of the
Lord, He will see that we have all necessary food

and clothing and raiment. It is a promise of the Lord.
—*Sermons in Outlines*

CONFESSING CHRIST

Matthew 10:32

The text is greatly emphasized by the circumstances of its utterance.

I. THE OBJECT TO BE CONFESSED.
- A. Not our good works, church membership, or worthy desires and purposes.
- B. Not some remarkable experience.
- C. But Christ as our Saviour and King, our trust in Him for pardon, and our obedience to Him as our Lawgiver.

II. TO WHOM THE CONFESSION IS TO BE MADE.
- A. To Christ — the heart.
- B. To men — "before men" (Romans 10:9,10). Do not hesitate from any cause. Remember:
    1. Christ requires it.
    2. He knows all about you.
    3. He wants to use your confession.

III. THE MANNER OF CONFESSING.
- A. By words; "with the mouth confession is made unto salvation."
- B. By acts; the ordinances and an upright life.

IV. THE PROMISE TO THOSE CONFESSING.
    They shall be confessed before the Father.
- A. Confessed now, which means forgiveness, reconciliation and unspeakably rich blessings in the life that now is.
- B. Confessed hereafter; received into glory; welcomed by the King in His beauty; "Come ye blessed of my Father."

V. How SIMPLE THE REQUIREMENT, How WONDERFUL
THE REWARD!

—Revival Sermons in Outline

THE EASY YOKE AND THE LIGHT BURDEN

For my yoke is easy, and My burden is light (Matthew 11:30).

I. THE YOKE OF CHRIST IS EASY, and His burden is light,
because we bear it with the approbation of conscience.
A burden which does not consist of sin is never heavy.

II. THIS YOKE IS EASY because it is borne in love.

III. CHRIST'S YOKE IS EASY and His burden is light because
it is borne with the help of the Spirit of God.

IV. CHRIST'S WORDS ARE TRUE because His burden becomes lighter the longer it is borne.

V. CHRIST'S YOKE IS EASY and His burden light because
we are sustained under it by a good hope.

A. Heaven and endless happiness is reserved for us.

—Three Hundred Outlines on the New Testament

THE PRESENCE OF JESUS

. . . Jesus went unto them, walking on the sea . . .
(Matthew 14:25-33).

I. THE PROBLEM OF HIS PRESENCE

"They were troubled." "They cried out for fear."
They did not recognize Jesus. He is always present.
He is with us always. We should always be able to
recognize Him and be willing to honor Him everywhere.

II. THE PROOF OF HIS PRESENCE

Jesus assured the disciples of His presence with the
same clear voice that they had often heard. He said

"Be of good cheer; it is I; be not afraid." Hear the voice of Jesus who comes to us just when we need Him most.

III. The Permission of His Presence

There was doubt in the heart of Peter, and Jesus gave him permission to walk on the water and to come to Him, but Peter's faith failed when he took his eyes off Jesus and saw the boisterous waves. Jesus is willing to be tried.

IV. The Power of His Presence

When Peter began to sink, he cried unto Jesus, "Lord, save me." Jesus stretched forth His hand and lifted the disciple out of trouble and calmed the waves. Jesus has power to control nature. He has all power and will manifest it to save the people. Call on Him.

V. The Praise of His Presence

"They that were in the ship came and worshipped him, saying, Of a truth thou art the Son of God." Hearts of praise should be lifted to Jesus for all that He is to our weak and failing lives. Praise Him. Worship Him. Love Him. Live in the presence of Jesus and allow Him to give blessings.

—Sermons in Outline

GREAT FAITH

O woman, great is thy faith; be it unto thee even as thou wilt (Matthew 15:28).

"Faith is the substance of things hoped for, the evidence of things not seen."

I. "Great Faith" Leads to Great Undertakings

It was a great undertaking for this woman to come to Christ.

II. "GREAT FAITH" BEGETS GREAT EXPECTATIONS
She expected the Saviour to heal her daughter. We often expect no great results from our labors, because we have not this great faith.

III. "GREAT FAITH" AWAKENS GREAT EARNESTNESS
She cried, and fell at His feet and worshiped Him. Look at the earnestness of Knox, Luther, Wesley, etc. They had great faith.

IV. "GREAT FAITH" CONQUERS GREAT DIFFICULTIES
First it is said, "He answered her not a word." But she kept on. Next He said He was not sent but to the lost sheep of the house of Israel. Still she is not discouraged. Next He said, "It was not meet to take the children's bread and cast it to the dogs." She answered, "Truth O Lord," etc. What difficulties have not been overcome by men of undaunted courage and faith!

V. "GREAT FAITH" ACHIEVES GREAT VICTORIES
"Be it unto thee even as thou wilt" and her daughter was made whole (Mark 9:23; Matthew 17:20; Hebrews 11:30-40).   —100 *Sermon Outlines*

THE SECRET OF POWER

Then came the disciples to Jesus apart, and said, Why could not we cast him out? And Jesus said unto them, Because of your unbelief (Matthew 17:19, 20).

We have success enough in Christian work to assure us that we possess a treasure, and failures enough to make us feel how weak are the earthen vessels that hold it.

I. WE HAVE AN UNVARYING POWER.
A. We have a Gospel that never can grow old.
B. We have an abiding Spirit.
C. We have a Lord the same yesterday, to-day, and forever.

II. The Condition of Exercising This Power Is Faith.

With such a force at our command, a force that could shake the mountains and break the rocks, how can we think of failure? Christ throws the disciples back decisively upon themselves as solely responsible.

We have received all spiritual gifts in proportion to our capacity, and our capacity is mainly settled by our faith.

The same faith has a natural operation upon ourselves which tends to fit us for casting out the evil spirit. It makes us simple, fearless, strong.

Faith has power over men who see it. There is a magnetism in the sight of a brother's faith which few can resist.

III. Our Faith Is Ever Threatened by Subtle Unbelief.

Our activity in spreading the Gospel tends to become mechanical.

The atmosphere of scornful disbelief which surrounds us makes our faith falter.

IV. Our Faith Can Only Be Maintained by Constant Devotion and Rigid Self-Denial.

It is no holiday task to cast out devils. Self-indulgent men will never do it.

COLD LOVE

Because iniquity shall abound, the love of many shall wax cold (Matthew 24:12).

  I. The Case—Waxing cold
 II. The Cause—Abounding in iniquity
III. The Cure—The warmth of God's love

THE SERVANT OF THE LORD

Well done, thou good and faithful servant (Matthew 25:21).

I. A Servant.

A servant is one who exerts himself for the benefit of another.

A servant of the Lord is one who exerts every part of his being for the good of the cause of the Lord.

II. A Good Servant.

A good servant of the Lord is one who knows what to do and when to do it and how to do it for the glory of the Lord.

A good servant is one who is efficient and effective, fearless and forceful, earnest and energetic.

III. A Faithful Servant.

A faithful servant of the Lord is one who toils on and on without failure, or discouragement, or hesitancy for the good of the kingdom.

IV. A Trusted Servant.

"I will make thee ruler over many things." Great servants of the Lord have had humble beginnings. As they have served and gained strength and ability, the Lord has placed them in greater and greater places of responsibility. The person who is trustworthy in small things is likely to be put in trust with larger things.

V. A Commended Servant.

"Well done." It is like the Lord to praise the person who is good and faithful. He will not only commend such persons and encourage them, but will reward them.

May we all be such good and faithful servants that we may win the "Well done" from the Lord in this life and the life to come.

—Sermon Outlines

CHRISTIAN GIVING

(Luke 6:38)

I. The Whole Basis of Christianity Rests Upon This One Word—*Give*

    A. God gave His Son   (John 3:16)

    B. Jesus gave Himself   (Galatians 2:20)

    C. We should imitate God, and give, as He gave
       (1) ourselves (II Corinthians 8:5), (2) our sub-
       stance (Proverbs 3:9, 10).

 II. How We Are to Give
    A. Out of a perfect heart   (I Chronicles 29:9)
    B. Willingly   (II Corinthians 9:7)
    C. Abundantly   (Luke 6:38)

III. Some Who Gave of Their Substance to the Lord,
    and Were Blessed Thereby—
    A. Abraham   (Hebrews 7:1, 2)
    B. The woman that was a sinner (Luke 7:37)
    C. The poor widow   (Luke 21:1, 4)

IV. As We Give to God and His Cause, so We May
    Expect He Will Give to Us
          (Luke 6:38; Proverbs 11:24)

THY WILL BE DONE

Thy will be done as in heaven, so on earth (Luke 11:2).

The chief meaning of this petition is not that we should
suffer, but that we should act. With earnest and firm
resolve we should set ourselves upon doing that which
our own consciences tell us God would have us to do.
But let us consider, first, its bearing upon suffering.

  I. Though This Is a Part of the Meaning of the Peti-
    tion, It Is But a Small Part.
    A. God has so constituted the world as for trouble to
       form part of our common lot, falling upon some
       but lightly and at distant intervals, and visiting
       others blow upon blow until their hearts are
       bowed down and overclouded with sorrow.
    B. Our reason tells us that to submit to God's law is
       wise. But when our own turn comes to suffer,
       our will rises against God, and it is faith only

that can make us say, "Thy will be done" — faith in God's love, in Christ's salvation, and in the promised glory of Christ's kingdom.

II. THE MORE IMPORTANT MEANING OF THE PETITION IS "THY WILL BE DONE" ACTIVELY BY US, BY OUR EARNESTLY SETTING OURSELVES TO LIVE A LIFE OF FAITH.

    A. This is the more important for two reasons:

        1. Because it is the true meaning of the petition, not "Thy will be endured," but "Thy will be done."

        2. It is to be done as in heaven.

        3. But there is no suffering in heaven.

        4. Besides, the doing of God's will includes the bearing of it as the cause includes the effect.

        5. All we can do is by the grace of God. To obtain this grace we must pray.

III. GOD'S WILL MUST NOT ONLY BE DONE, BUT DONE AS HIS WILL.

    A. How this is to be is to be seen by our Lord's example.

    B. That is the hardest thing of all — to do God's will.

        1. We can because our natures have been transformed, all selfishness and earthly longing removed, and the image of God once again restored in our defiled and sin-corrupted breasts.

—Three Hundred Outlines on the New Testament

THE STRAIT GATE

Strive to enter in at the strait gate; for many, I say unto you, will seek to enter in, but shall not be able (Luke 13:24).

I. THE GATE WHICH IT IS MOST DESIRABLE TO ENTER.

    A. Because it is the gate of the City of Refuge.

    B. Because it is the gate of a home.

C. Because it leads to a blessed feast.

D. Because the loss of those outside the gate is too terrible.

II. There Is a Crowd of People Who Will Seek to Enter in and Will Not Be Able.

There is a differance between seeking and striving.

A. Some are unable to enter in because the pride of life will not let them.

B. Some are unable to enter because they seek to take sin with them.

C. Some are unable to enter because they want to postpone the matter until to-morrow.

D. Some think they are in and have mistaken the outside for the inside.

—*Three Hundred Outlines on the New Testament*

TWO WORLDS

But Abraham said, Son, remember that thou in thy lifetime receivedst thy good things, and likewise Lazarus evil things; but now he is comforted and thou art tormented (Luke 16:25).

The lesson is, the man who seeks enjoyment in this life as his chief end must suffer in the next life, and he who endures suffering in this life for righteousness' sake shall be happy in the next.

I. What Are the Good Things Which the Rich Man Received Here for Which He Must Be Tormented Hereafter?

A. The worldly man derives a more intense physical enjoyment from this world's goods, than does the the child of God. In the past history of mankind the great positions and the great incomes, as a general rule, have not been in the hands of simple and penitent men. Besides, how often does it happen that a fine physical constitution, health and vigour, are given to the worldling and denied to the child of God.

B. The worldly man derives more enjoyment from sin and suffers less from it in this life than does the child of God. The really renewed man cannot enjoy sin. The days of a stupid and impenitent man glide by with no twinges of conscience. But is it right, is it just that this state of things should last for ever? Ought it not to be reversed?

II. THE PRACTICAL LESSONS WHICH FOLLOW FROM THIS SUBJECT ARE —

A. No man can have his good things, in other words his chief pleasures, in both worlds. God and this world are in antagonism.

B. Every man must make his choice whether he will have his good things now or hereafter.

C. It is the duty and wisdom of every man to let this world and to seek his good things hereafter.

—*Three Hundred Outlines on the New Testament*

PETER'S SIN

And the Lord turned and looked upon Peter (Luke 22:61).

The sins of God's people are noted in Scripture to show us first, that we must cut off all man worship in the church of Christ; second, to show us that it was not through works, but entirely through Christ, that even the most eminent and faithful of God's servants were chosen; third, that we may learn to know the evil of the unbelief that is within us, and that we are altogether dependent upon the grace of God.

I. MARK HOW THE STRONGEST ARE WEAK IN THEIR STRONGEST POINT.

A. Peter's courage and election were the very points in which he failed.

II. PETER SINNED AGAINST LIGHT — BRIGHT AND FULLY REVEALED LIGHT.
   A. Jesus was before him when he denied Him.
   B. So do we all sin against light and in the presence of light.

III. REMEMBER HOW CHRIST HAD FOREWARNED PETER.
   A. He not only saw Peter manifesting his zeal and devotion, but He beheld that fierce and awful enemy who was to assail him.

IV. THIS LOOKING SHOWED THAT WHILE THE EYE OF CHRIST WAS RESTING ON THE FAILINGS OF PETER, IT WAS PENETRATING THE INNERMOST RECESSES OF HIS HEART.
   A. That look of Jesus, although it was like a sharp sword piercing the very heart of Peter, was also the healing balm, the life-giving tide, the refreshing rain which came into the soul of Peter.

—Three Hundred Outlines on the New Testament

SPIRITUAL WORSHIP

But the hour cometh, and now is, when the true worshipers shall worship the Father in spirit and in truth: for the Father seeketh such to worship him (John 4:23).

I. WE MUST WORSHIP GOD IN HIS TRUE NATURE
   A. Personality
   B. Unity

II. WE MUST WORSHIP HIM IN THE RIGHT RELATION
   A. Our Father
   B. Reconciled

III. WE MUST WORSHIP HIM IN THE RIGHT MANNER
   A. In spirit—opposed to place, ceremonies, formality
   B. In truth—through the medium of Christ the truth

—Pulpit Germs

CHRIST, THE SINCERE SHEPHERD

I am the good shepherd . . . (John 10:11).

These are the words of Jesus. He is our Good Shepherd. We are His sheep. See what He does as the Good Shepherd of our souls.

I. HE LEARNS US

"I know my sheep." "He calleth his own sheep by name." As the Good Shepherd of our souls, the Lord Jesus Christ knows our names, our dispositions, our desires, our aims, our abilities, our faults, the degrees of consecration, and all that is to be known.

II. HE LOVES US

"I lay down my life for the sheep." That tells the extent of the love of Christ for sinners. "Christ died for our sins according to the scriptures." "God commendeth his love toward us, in that while we are yet sinners, Christ died for us." He loves us. His love is supreme and eternal.

III. HE LEADS US

"Leadeth them out." "When he putteth forth his own sheep, he goeth before them." What a joy and satisfaction to follow such Leader! We follow Him for we know His voice. He leads us by His presence, by His words, and by impression. He is the Good Shepherd, and His own should follow Him.

IV. HE LONGS FOR US

"I am known of mine." He longs that we should know Him. "Learn of me." As His sheep we "know his voice" and follow Him because we know He desires that we be near Him. He longs to protect His own from dangerous enemies, longs to lead His own to green pastures, and longs to feed His own with rich food from heaven.

V. HE LIVES FOR US

"I am come that they might have life, and that they might have it more abundantly." "Because I live, ye shall live also." "I give unto them eternal life; and they shall never perish, neither shall any man pluck them out of my hand." He lives for us. In Him we may live forever.

—*Sermons in Outline*

THE GOOD SHEPHERD

I am the Good Shepherd (John 10:11).

When Our Lord calls Himself the Good Shepherd, is He using a title which has lost its value since He has ceased to live visibly upon the earth? This title has a true meaning for Christians, and an attractive power which is all its own. To enter into the full force of this image, we must know something really of ourselves, and something really of our Saviour.

I. As the Good Shepherd, He Knows His Sheep.

He knows us individually, not merely as we seem to be, but as we are. It is because He thus knows us that He is able to help, guide and feed us.

II. He Has a Perfect Sympathy With Each.

He is not a hard guardian, without any sort of feeling for our individual difficulties, yet this sympathy is guided by perfect prudence. The Good Shepherd has proportioned our duties, our trials, our advantages, our drawbacks, to our real needs, capacities and characters.

III. He Is Disinterested Above All, As the Good Shepherd.

He seeks not ours, but us. He gains nothing by watching, guiding, feeding such as us. He gave His life for the sheep. He gave it once for all over nineteen centuries ago; but His death is just as powerful to deliver us from the onset of the wolf as then. Self-sacrifice such as that on Calvary does not lose its virtue by the lapse of years.

—Three Hundred Outlines on the New Testament

THE THREEFOLD WORK OF THE HOLY SPIRIT

(John 16:7-11)

I. To Convince of Sin
II. To Convince of Righteousness
III. To Convince of Judgment to Come

THE BELIEVER'S POSITION

Given out of the world — — —   (John 17:6)
Sent into the world — — — —   (John 17:18)
Left in the world — — — — —   (John 17:11)
Not of the world — — — — —   (John 17:14)
Hated by the world — — — —   (John 17:14)
Kept from the evil of the world —   (John 17:15)

—Pegs for Preachers

A PRAYER-MEETING IN THE APOSTOLIC TIMES

(Acts 12:5)

Peter had continued in prayer for the Church, and now the Church continues in prayer for him. There is blessed cooperation in the mystical body. It is a proof we are members of this body, if we bear one another's sorrows. Not pity, or condole, or promise only, but really put our shoulder to the burden.

I. Observe, in This Case They Confined Their Efforts
   to Prayer

Sometimes we find ourselves in such a position that we can do nothing but pray. Like Israel at the Red Sea: no power of theirs can make a passage through the waters, or defeat the oncoming legions; they can only wait on God. Or like Daniel in the lions' den, or Elijah when the rain was withheld. For such times we have a promise, "Ask, and ye shall receive."

II. Observe, They Continued in This Effort

It was no formal or heartless prayer-meeting. They must have possessed strong faith. The case seemed hopeless. Tomorrow is fixed for Peter's death (verse 6). The hate of Herod is known to be malignant. James the apostle had been already slain.

III. They Reaped the Benefit

The answer filled them with amazement.

The answer was superabundant.

Perhaps they had not prayed for his deliverance that night, or for his deliverance at all, but that he might glorify God in the fire.

The answer was speedy.

—*Stems and Twigs*

A LIFE OF FAITH

. . . *as it is written, The just shall live by faith* (Romans 1:17).

Faith is essential to all life. Without faith it is impossible to please God. This text shows that faith is the source, the support, and the success of life.

I. Faith is the Source of Life

"By faith." Only by faith in the Lord Jesus Christ can one attain unto eternal life. It is believe and live. "Believe on the Lord Jesus Christ, and thou shalt be saved." "He that believeth on the Son hath eternal life." Eternal life is possible only by grace through faith in the Lord Jesus Christ. Real life begins with faith in Christ.

II. FAITH IS THE SUPPORT OF LIFE

"Shall live by faith." Faith in the Lord and in His power to help is the support of life. "Who is he that overcometh the world, but he that believeth that Jesus is the Son of God?" Faith is the force that supports life and sustains life unto the end. Faith enriches life. Faith enlarges life. Faith enables life. Faith increases life.

III. FAITH IS THE SUCCESS OF LIFE

"The righteous shall live by faith." Faith is the force that leads on to righteousness. It is the power that will appropriate the righteousness of Christ for the life of the individual in the world. Believe in Christ, appropriate His grace, and follow Him is the only way to succeed in the Christian life.

By faith live and serve. "Without faith it is impossible to please God."

—SERMONS IN OUTLINE
Jerome O. Williams

THE PROOF OF GOD'S LOVE

But God commendeth His love toward us, in that, while we were yet sinners, Christ died for us (Romans 5:8).

In broad and striking contrast with the comparative poverty of our human love, Paul sets the greatness and the wonder of God's love to man.

I. GOD DOES NOT ASK US TO TAKE HIS LOVE SIMPLY ON TRUST.

A. To doubt His love would be an affront to the reason as well as a dishonour to the heart.

B. Our faith is not vain in the sense of being unsupported by proofs.

II. What Is the Proof?

A. Christ died for us.

1. The death of Christ was the manifestation of the infinite love of God to man, and was designed to prove it to the world. It was not necessary for Christ to die to make God love us, but Christ died to show that God already loved us.

B. While we were yet sinners He died for us.

1. If He had died for good men it would have been an amazing act of love; but it was more.

2. A profound sense of sin is always associated with a profound realization of the greatness of the love of God.

III. The Cross of Christ Is a Present Reality.

A. The Apostle does not say God has proved His love towards, as if it were something away in the past; but he says it is a proof going on still.

1. The Cross speaks to the heart of man with the same tenderness and power as it did to the eye-witnesses of the love and sorrow of His passion and death.

—*Three Hundred Outlines on the New Testament*

NO CONDEMNATION

There is therefore now no condemnation to them which are in Christ Jesus, who walk not after the flesh, but after the Spirit (Romans 8:1).

The truth here declared follows from the position taken up by Paul in the preceding portion of his epistle.

I. There Is No Condemnatory Sentence in Execution Against Christians Now.

A. Believers in Jesus Christ still sin, and their sins are noticed by God, and God is displeased with them; but He does not treat them as criminals, but as children.

1. No sentence of condemnation is being executed outwardly and none is being executed inwardly.

2. Being justified by faith we have peace with God.

II. THERE IS NO SENTENCE OF CONDEMNATION RECORDED FOR EXECUTION.

A. The disciple of Christ is not reproved but pardoned, and his pardon is full and complete.

1. In God's book there is no recognition whatever of the sins He has forgiven.

2. He does not throw our sins on the surface of the sea to appear again like bread cast on the waters, but buries them in the depths.

III. THE ABSENCE OF ALL CONDEMNATION IS ACCOUNTED FOR BY THAT WHICH CHRIST IS TO THE SOUL THAT RELIES UPON HIM.

A. Christ is the Lamb of God that taketh away the the sin of the world.

1. Simple trust appropriates the sin-offering.

B. He is the High Priest who ever liveth to make intercession for us, and faith in Jesus gives us a personal interest in that intercession.

C. But how may I know whether I am trusting the true Christ, the Christ of God?

1. The reality of our reliance in the Christ of God is proved by the character and style of our life.

2. Jesus Christ leads all His disciples to walk not after the flesh but after the Spirit.

—*Three Hundred Outlines on the New Testament*

    D. *He maketh intercession for us* (I John 2:1; Hebrews 7:25; 9:24).

II. THE COMFORT THE BELIEVER DERIVES FROM THESE TRUTHS

    Who is he that condemneth?

    A. *Our hearts cannot condemn us* (Romans 8:1).

    B. *The world cannot condemn us* (v. 33; 4:25).

    C. *The devil cannot condemn us* — He is "the accuser of the brethren," but Christ ascended on high and now exercises kingly power even over the devil.

    D. *The Father will not condemn us* — For Christ is our Advocate with the Father.

    Happy state, to be free from condemnation!

—100 Sermon Outlines

VICTORY

More than conquerors (Romans 8:37).

The key-note of the text is "Victory." It is the characteristic of all God's works, that whatever He does, He does abundantly. There is always something in excess; a David's cup that runneth over, or a Joseph's bough which runneth over the wall.

Every miracle was done overflowingly. The lame man not only walked but leaped. When the daughter of Jairus was raised to life, Jesus commands that "something be given her to eat"; and the very fragments of His feedings are "twelve baskets full."

Christ came into this world "that we might have life, more abundantly." The life in union with Him is a truer and a greater life than unfallen life, than any angel's life could ever have been. "We are more than conquerors."

I. CONSIDER HOW CHRIST WAS "MORE THAN CONQUEROR."

    A. In His death.

        1. A prayer for His enemies.

  2. A provision of filial tenderness for His mother.
  3. A free pardon to a sinner.
  4. The largess of a kingdom with a royal hand.
  5. These were the achievements of the dying man, Christ Jesus. "More than conqueror."

 B. In His rising.
  1. The victory would have been complete if that body had come forth the same, but He did more.
  2. The body was more beautiful, more spiritual than the body which was laid in the grave.

 C. In His ascension and exaltation.
  1. He ascends but does not leave His followers to weep — for He is more with them than before — He is exalted, and none are orphaned. He is "more than conqueror."

II. THE BELIEVER IS "MORE THAN CONQUEROR."

 A. In the contest with Satan, God undertakes that His people shall not be overcome, and more, that they shall overcome and put the enemy in fear. "He will flee from you."

 B. Then a sin overcome necessarily becomes a virtue.
  1. Satan is foiled with his own weapons, and Israel enriched with the spoils of Egypt.
  2. That too much speaking will become eloquence for Christ, that temper will make zeal.

 C. The Christian would not exchange the dark memories of sorrow and bereavement for the sunniest of the world's hours.
  1. There was so much of Christ in them, so much of a tranquil mind, so much of heaven, that he comes out of the sorrow "more than conqueror."
  2. And so when we die, like a ship, at high tide, pressing full-sailed into port, "an entrance is ministered unto us abundantly" into the king-

dom. The world conquers— the Church is "more than conqueror."

WHAT CHRISTIANS SHALL BE

Eye hath not seen, nor ear heard . . . the things which God hath prepared for them that love him (I Corinthians 2:9).

I. They Shall Be Changed (I Corinthians 15:51, 52)
II. They Shall Be Caught Up (I Thessalonians 4:17)
III. They Shall Be Like Christ (I John 3:2)
IV. They Shall Appear With Christ (Colossians 3:4)
V. They Shall Be Judges (I Corinthians 6:2, 3)
VI. They Shall Be Priests (Revelation 20:6; 1:6; 5:10)
VII. They Shall Be With Christ Forever (I Thessalonians 4:17, 18)

—Treasures of Bible Truth
William H. Schweinfurth

BELONGING TO CHRIST

And ye are Christ's (I Corinthians 3:23).

I. Here Is Ownership, With the Idea of Responsibility. We as believers are Christ's—

A. By creation.
B. By providence.
C. By donation.
D. By redemption.
E. By conquest.
F. By surrender.

II. Here Is Relationship with the Idea of Privilege.

This relationship is expressed in various ways in the Scriptures.

A. We are His sheep (John 10:1-15).
B. We are His servants (Acts 4:29).

C. We are His friends (John 15:13-15).

D. We are His brothers (Matthew 12:48; Mark 3:35).

E. We are His bride (John 3:29; Revelation 21:2).

F. We are His body (Romans 12:4, 5; Ephesians 4:15, 16).

G. We are one in spirit with Christ (I Corinthians 6:17).

H. "It doth not yet appear what we shall be: but we know that when he shall appear, we shall be like him, for we shall see him as he is" (I John 3:2).

—Revival Sermons in Outline

BOUGHT WITH A PRICE

Ye are not your own, for ye are bought with a price: therefore glorify God in your body, and in your spirit, which are God's (I Corinthians 6:19, 20).

How strangely sounds this sentence in the ears of human pride! With what infinite wonder does it fill the natural man!

I. WE NOTICE FIRST THE GREAT FACT ASSERTED IN THE TEXT, THAT WE ARE PURCHASED, AND THE POSITION INTO WHICH WE ARE BROUGHT BECAUSE OF THAT PURCHASE.

A. We are redeemed by the precious blood of Christ, and therefore we are not our own.

II. WHAT IS THE COURSE OF CONDUCT WHICH A CONSIDERATION OF SUCH POSITION IS CALCULATED TO INDUCE US TO PURSUE?

A. Let your devotedness to God be entire; glorify God in your bodies, in your intellect, in all your powers.

B. Let your devotedness be benevolent. Spend yourselves in energetic endeavours for the conversion of your fellows, and for the spread of the Gospel among you. There is an influence for good as well as an influence for evil.

C. Let your devotedness to God be consummated now — now, when the conflict between sense and faith, between the ceremonial and the spiritual, between the idolatrous and the ever-living, has commenced, and a thousand voices of the universe are pealing out the challenge: "Who is on the Lord's side?

—*Three Hundred Outlines on the New Testament*

THE CHRISTIAN RACE

I Corinthians 9:24

I. THREE CLASSES.
  A. Non-competitors (Philippians 3:18, 19; Hebrews 2:3).
  B. Failing competitors (I Corinthians 3:15).
  C. Winning competitors (II Timothy 4:7, 8).

II. CONDITIONS FOR COMPETITION.
  A. Must be a citizen (Ephesians 2:19).
  B. Blameless (Romans 8:1).
  C. Must offer himself (Romans 12:1).
  D. Must be accepted (Ephesians 1:6).

III. CONDITIONS IN THE RACE.
  A. He must start right (John 10:9).
  B. Keep to the course (John 14:6).
  C. Must strip (Hebrews 12:1).

IV. CAUSES OF FAILURE.
  A. Turning or backsliding (Psalm 78:9; Acts 7:39).
  B. Tripping or careless walking (John 11:10).
  C. Tired or weary walking (Malachi 1:13; Isaiah 40:31).

—*Tools for the Master's Work*
J. ELLIS

TEMPTATION

*There hath no temptation taken you but such as is common
to man: but God is faithful, who will not suffer you to be
tempted above that ye are able; but will with the temptation
also make a way to escape, that ye may be able to bear it*
(I Corinthians 10:13).

The apostle has just been warning against too much
self-confidence; he now speaks against the opposite faults,
too much downheartedness and despondency.

I. THERE IS A PRECISE CORRESPONDENCE BETWEEN
   STRENGTH AND TRIAL
   A. The temptation is proportioned to the power of
      resistance.
   B. Do not think that there is something hard and
      heavy and worse than all the past to come: the
      burden is made for the back.

II. THE VERY SAME DIVINE ACT MAKES BOTH THE TRIAL
    AND THE WAY TO GET OUT OF IT.
    A. God tempts us only in the way of testing us, and
       He points a way of escape.
       1. We are never brought into a blind alley; it is
          a thoroughfare, and we can get out if we
          please; with the Egyptians on this side, and the
          sea on that, God will clear the waters of the
          deep to make a way.

III. THIS MUST BE SO UNLESS GOD MAKE HIMSELF A LIAR.

I wish to put it strongly. If it were not so, men would
have a right to turn upon God and to say, "Thou hast
deceived me."

God does not force His help upon us; but nothing will
come to us that we shall not be able to baffle and beat,
so long as we have His strength for ours.

   —Three Hundred Outlines on the New Testament

HOLY SPIRIT AND HIS WORK

The Spirit of the living God (II Corinthians 3:3).

God deals with men through His Holy Spirit in this age.

I. How He Works FOR Man.
  - A. By applying the Word (Acts 28:28; I Timothy 3:16).
  - B. By promulgating the Word (Acts 2:4; Acts 13:2).
  - C. By interpreting the Word (John 16:13; Acts 8:39).

II. How He Works IN Man.
  - A. In conviction (John 16:8).
  - B. In enlightenment (John 14:26).
  - C. In regeneration (John 3:5).

III. How He Works BY Man.
  - A. Man is prepared for work (Elisha for Israel).
  - B. Work is prepared for man (Nineveh for Jonah).
  - C. Work is revealed to man (Exodus to Moses).

IV. How He Works WITH Man.
  - A. His comforting presence (John 16:7).
  - B. His powerful assistance (John 14:12).
  - C. His sanctifying indwelling (Romans 15:16).

—*Tools for the Master's Work*

J. Ellis

MIRRORS OF CHRIST

But we all, with open face beholding as in a glass the glory of the Lord, are changed into the same image from glory to glory, even as by the Spirit of the Lord (II Corinthians 3:18).

The idea which Paul here announces is, that they who are much in Christ's presence become mirrors of Him, reflecting more and more permanently His image until they themselves perfectly resemble Him. This assertion rests upon a well known law of our nature. Our duty, then, if we would be transformed into the image of Christ, is plain.

I. WE MUST ASSOCIATE WITH HIM; WE MUST MAKE HIM
   OUR MOST CONSTANT COMPANION.
   A. We must not reflect Him in an occasional inter-
      mittent way, but steadily and continually.
   B. We must live with Him.
II. WE MUST BE CAREFUL TO TURN FULLY ROUND TO
    CHRIST, SO AS TO GIVE A FULL AND FAIR REFLECTION
    OF HIM. We must not turn only half round, so as
    still to let other images fall on us.
III. WE MUST STAND IN HIS PRESENCE WITH OPEN UN-
     VEILED FACE.
   A. We may wear a veil in the world, refusing to re-
      flect it, but when we return to the Lord we must
      uncover our face.
      1. A covered mirror reflects nothing.
      2. Perfect beauty may stand before it, but the
         napkin shows no sign, offers no response.
IV. IT REDUCES ITSELF TO THIS.
   A. Be much in the presence of Christ.
   B. Be so honestly enamored of Him that you will find
      Him everywhere, and that your thoughts will fall
      back to Him as often as the engagements of life
      permit.
V. HERE IS SOMETHING WE CAN DO FOR CHRIST: WE CAN
   REFLECT HIM.
   A. By reflecting Him we shall certainly extend the
      knowledge of Him.
   B. Many who do not look at Him look at you.
      —*Three Hundred Outlines on the New Testament*

DELIVERANCE

For we that are in this tabernacle do groan, being burdened . . .
(II Corinthians 5:4).

I. THE CHRISTIAN'S PRESENT CONDITION
   A. The body is a tent — *Movable*

B. It is earthly in its elements — *Tendencies*
C. It is mortal — *There are rents in it already*
D. The soul is a sojourner in it.

II. HIS CIRCUMSTANCES — "BURDENED"
A. By the vicissitudes of life
B. By persecutions
C. By temptations
D. By the remains of sin

III. HIS DESIRE — "GROAN"
A. For deliverance
B. For a permanent house — *Home*

—Pulpit Germs

THE OLD AND THE NEW

Old things have passed away, behold all things are become new (II Corinthians 5:17).

I. THE OLD
A. Spiritual darkness; blind in sin (Ephesians 4:18).
B. Satan's bond-servants (Proverbs 5:22; II Timothy 2:26).
C. Children of the devil (John 8:44).
D. Morally defiled (Isaiah 1:6; Mark 7:21, 22).
E. An evil conscience.
F. An unholy life. "Such were some of you" (I Corinthians 6:9, 10).
G. Pleasure in sin.
H. Without hope and without God in the world (Ephesians 2:12).

II. THE NEW
A. Eyes opened; heart enlightened (John 8:12; I John 1:6).
B. Free from the bondage of sin (Galatians 5:1).
C. Children of God (I John 3:1, 2).

D. Morally pure; affections sanctified (Matthew 5:8).

E. A good conscience (Acts 24:16; I John 3:21).

F. A holy life.

G. Pleasure in doing good. Joy in the service of Christ.

H. A lively hope of a blessed immortality (I Peter 1:3, 4).

—100 *Sermon Outlines*

A NEW CREATURE

If any man be in Christ, he is a new creature (II Corinthians 5:17).

It is important to understand what we are as Christians, not merely what we ought to be, or what we will be, but what we are. Our text declares what every Christian is. "If *any* man," no matter who, is a Christian, "he is a new creature."

I. HE IS NEW IN HIS RELATIONS TO GOD.

A. New in his relation to the law of God.

1. "He that believeth not is condemned already" (John 3:18).

2. "There is therefore now no condemnation to them who are in Christ Jesus" (Romans 8:1).

3. The convict is pardoned, and becomes a new man in relation to the law.

B. New in relation to the government of God.

1. "Aliens from the commonwealth of Israel" have become "no more strangers and foreigners, but fellow-citizens with the saints" (Ephesians 2:12, 19).

C. New in relation to the family of God.

1. Every Christian is "of the household of faith."

II. IF ANY MAN BE IN CHRIST HE IS NEW IN HIS RELATIONS TO HIS FELLOW-MAN.

A. A new man in responsibility.
1. "Now, then, we are ambassadors for Christ."
2. "He hath committed unto us the word of reconciliation" (II Corinthians 5:19, 20).
B. New in opportunity.
1. Before the Christian is an open door.
2. He can minister to sinning, suffering, sorrowing humanity.

III. IF ANY MAN BE IN CHRIST, HE IS A NEW CREATURE IN HIS EXPERIENCES.
A. There is an abiding consciousness of security.
B. The Christian is blessed in the thought that he is on the right side.
C. Hope is a precious element in this new experience.
D. Communion with God refreshes the soul.
E. The whole range of experience is touched by the indwelling Christ.

IV. IF ANY MAN BE IN CHRIST, HE IS A NEW CREATURE AT THE CENTER OF HIS BEING.
A. This new life may be repressed and undeveloped, but if any man be in Christ, the new life has been begotten in his soul.
B. This is fundamental — "Except a man be born again (or anew) he cannot see the kingdom of God."

V. WHAT A WONDERFUL NEWNESS IS OURS!
A. Seeing these things are so, what manner of men ought we to be?
B. Surely when any one unsaved comes to see what a Christian really is, he must desire to have these blessings, to be a new creature.
C. The door is open.
D. We as Christians must enter by faith into the riches of grace in Christ Jesus, and all shall be ours. *—Revival Sermons in Outline*

AMBASSADORS FOR CHRIST

Now then we are ambassadors for Christ . . . (II Corinthians 5:20).

God was in Christ reconciling the world to Himself, and Christ is in believers continuing this work of reconciliation. Study the following suggestions growing out of this subject and text.

I. THE PRESENCE OF CHRIST COMFORTS US

We believe in Christ, accept Him, confess Him as Saviour and Lord. We are then ready to enter into His service of reconciling others to the Father through Christ. It is a comfort to know that Christ will go with us. "Lo, I am with you."

II. THE PURPOSE OF CHRIST CONSTRAINS US

His purpose is to save the lost people of the earth. If we love Him we will have the same desire. His love and purpose constrains us.

III. THE PROGRAM OF CHRIST CHALLENGES US

The program of Christ extends to the full salvation of all the people of all nations of all the earth. It is the largest task known to men. It is great enough for the most ambitious.

IV. THE PERSON OF CHRIST COMPELS US

He stands by our side. He looks on when we do His will. He inspires us to our best. We see Him and feel compelled to do our best for Him. It is like the son when father looks on to assist.

V. THE POWER OF CHRIST COMPLETES US

Without Christ we can do nothing. In His strength we can do all things. We can be complete in Him. His power is available. Use it.

—Sermons in Outline
JEROME O. WILLIAMS

THE FRUIT OF THE SPIRIT

*But the fruit of the Spirit is love, joy, peace, longsuffering,
gentleness, goodness, faith, meekness, temperance* (Galatians
5:22, 23).

We have "the works of the flesh," but we do not read
of "the fruits of the Spirit," but in the singular number
— fruit.

The nine graces are one fruit.

I. ALL THE OTHER FRUITS OF THE SPIRIT ARE ONLY THE
EXPANSION OF THE FIRST.

A. Joy is love triumphing.

B. Peace is love resting.

C. Long-suffering is love under the great trials.

D. Gentleness is love under the little trials of life.

E. Goodness is love going forth into action.

F. Faith is love sitting and receiving back again to
its own bosom.

G. Meekness is love controlling the passions of the
mind.

H. Temperance, the same love subduing the passions
of the body.

The law of the Spirit is all contained in one word, and
the unity of the whole Christian character is "love." Fruit
is not fruit if it is not sweet. What is anything to God
until there is love in it? Therefore love stands first.

II. THERE IS A LAW OF GROWTH ABOUT THE SPIRIT OF GOD
IN A MAN.

A. This is as sure as the law which regulates the
growth and development of any plant.

1. This truth is wrapped up in the metaphor "the
fruit of the Spirit."

2. If there is not advance in the image of Christ,
it is because the work of the Holy Ghost is
obstructed, for the Spirit, in Himself, always
essentially grows.

III. TO BE FRUIT-BEARERS WE MUST BE ENGRAFTED INTO THE TRUE VINE.
  A. If there is one state more solemn than another it is the leafy state.
    1. What if Jesus, drawing nigh to any one of us and finding nothing but leaves, should punish the barrenness which is wilful by the barrenness which is judicial: "No man eat fruit of thee hereafter for ever"?

  —*Three Hundred Outlines on the New Testament*

PROGRESS IN GRACE

I. SAVED BY GRACE (Ephesians 2:8).
  A. We need to acquaint ourselves with the grace of God: that wonderful new thing that Christ revealed to men.
    1. He showed it long ago in His life, teaching, and death for sinners, but many still do not know anything about it: know no other way of holiness but by works of law.
  B. We need to verify in our own experience that a saving virtue resides in the grace of God.
    1. Let us try to realize what it means that the God we had offended by our sin, whom we had ignored by our indifference has ever been looking on us in love and planning to make us fit to enjoy Himself forever? Has the grace of God saved you from sin?
II. STANDING IN GRACE: established in it (Romans 5:2).
III. TAUGHT BY GRACE (Titus 2:12).
  A. We cannot possibly be affected by the grace of God without its having a revolutionary effect on our conduct.

IV. GROWING IN GRACE (II Peter 3:18).
   A. As the years go on we shall get larger and fuller views of God's grace.

V. SPEAKING IN GRACE (Colossians 4:6).
   A. We shall not be able to keep the blessing to ourselves; we shall speak of the grace of God and in the grace of God.
   B. Our way of speaking to others should give them some idea of how Christ spoke to men.
   C. Our conversation is to be always with grace, tempered with salt which saves from corruption.

VI. MINISTERING GRACE (Ephesians 4:29).
   A. Our intercourse with others should be of such a character that it helps to form them also in the likeness of Christ.
   B. All our conduct towards others should tend to show them more and more of the beauty of the grace as revealed in Christ.

VII. WHO IS SUFFICIENT FOR THESE THINGS?
   We can neither receive nor show the grace of God in our own strength, but only through Christ's enabling, in answer to prayer.

—100 *Sermon Outlines*

THE SCOPE OF CHRISTIAN EXPERIENCE

For we are his workmanship, created in Christ Jesus unto good works . . . (Ephesians 2:10).

The soul's sublime experience is salvation by grace through faith in the Lord Jesus Christ. The fulness of this gracious experience has a wide scope.

I. THIS EXPERIENCE HAS THE UPWARD REACH
   "We are his workmanship." We become new creatures in Christ by the grace of God. It is the work of God

the Father. The experience is with the Father, the Lord Jesus Christ and the Holy Spirit. Faith must reach upward and take hold of the grace of God by faith.

II. THIS EXPERIENCE HAS THE INWARD REACH

"Created in Christ Jesus." In conviction the soul realizes it is in sin. In repentance it turns away from sin and by faith unto Christ. In regeneration the soul is made new in Christ and becomes a new creation with new hopes, new desires, new thoughts, and new purposes, and new determinations.

III. THIS EXPERIENCE HAS THE OUTWARD REACH

"Unto good works." God has a purpose in salvation. The saved soul will reach out for others for Christ. It will desire to become a laborer with God for a lost world.   —*Sermons in Outline*
                                      JEROME O. WILLIAMS

CHRIST'S RELATION TO THE BELIEVER

(Ephesians 2:14-22)

I. CHRIST OUR PEACE (verses 14-15)
II. CHRIST OUR RECONCILIATION (verses 16-17)
III. CHRIST OUR MEDIATOR (verses 18-19)
IV. CHRIST OUR FOUNDATION (verses 20-22)
                                      —*Lorraine Shearman*

CHRISTIAN CHARACTER

Be ye kind one to another, tenderhearted, forgiving one another, even as God for Christ's sake hath forgiven you (Ephesians 4:32).

This text gives the extent, the experience, the expression, and the best example of Christian character.

I. THE EXTENT OF CHRISTIAN CHARACTER.

"Be ye kind." When a person is born again by the Spirit of God, he becomes a new creature in Christ. The inherent nature of this life will then become gentle, gracious, kind, good and benevolent. Such characteristics will dominate the entire life. These characteristics make up the real Christian personality.

II. THE EXPERIENCE IN CHRISTIAN CHARACTER.

"Be ye . . . tenderhearted." In its relations to others, the Christian character is easily moved to love, to pity, to sorrow, to sympathy. Such life will be able to place itself in the position of others and feel as they feel.

It will move with compassion for others as Jesus was moved.

It will quickly lend a helping hand to the person in need.

It will spend itself for others.

III. THE EXPRESSION OF CHRISTIAN CHARACTER.

"Forgiving one another." Christian character will readily express itself toward others in being willing to forgive those who sin against it.

A forgiving spirit is Christlike, for on the Cross Christ prayed for those who crucified Him, saying, "Father, forgive them; for they know not what they do."

Jesus taught that His followers should be willing to forgive a limitless number of times. Christian character expresses itself in willingness to forgive.

IV. THE EXAMPLE OF CHRISTIAN CHARACTER.

"Even as God for Christ's sake hath forgiven you." The example of God the Father, is here held up as the ideal for the Christian. This is the most sublime ideal. This is the highest example of Christian character. It is the highest and holiest ideal and should be before every Christian.

THE CHRIST LIFE

For me to live is Christ, and to die is gain (Philippians 1:21).

I. A LIFE OF OBEDIENCE (Acts 9:6; Hebrews 10:9)

II. A LIFE OF SERVICE (I Corinthians 9:22)

III. A LIFE OF POWER (Matthew 28:18; Philippians 4:13)

IV. A LIFE OF SACRIFICE (John 15:13; Philippians 3:7)

V. A LIFE OF SEPARATION (II Corinthians 6:14-18; Hebrews 7:26)

VI. A LIFE OF SUFFERING (II Corinthians 4:10, 11)

VII. A LIFE OF VICTORY (Philippians 2:9, 10, 11; I Corinthians 15:57; Romans 8:37)

—*Treasures of Bible Truth*
WILLIAM H. SCHWEINFURTH

PAUL'S DESIRE IN PHILIPPIANS

To KNOW Christ — — — — Philippians 3:10
To WIN Christ — — — — — Philippians 3:8
To be CONFORMED to Christ — — Philippians 3:10
To MAGNIFY Christ — — — — Philippians 1:20
To be FOUND in Christ — — — Philippians 3:9
To REJOICE in Christ — — — Philippians 2:16
To be WITH Christ — — — — Philippians 1:23

—*Pegs for Preachers*

HOW TO KNOW CHRIST BETTER

That I may know him (Philippians 3:10).

To come to know Christ better was the first consuming desire of the heart of Paul after he met Him on the way to Damascus. We come to know Christ, first of all, by the new birth. Paul had passed this experience of grace. He applied himself definitely to know Christ better. All should long to know Him intimately. We make the following suggestions towards attaining this end:

I. SPEND MUCH TIME IN MEDITATION.

After Paul met Christ his first move was to go alone with God for a long season of meditation on the meaning of the experience. During these months of meditation he received the Gospel "by the revelation of Jesus Christ" (Galatians 1:12).

The Lord gave Paul the clearest and most perfect understanding of the Gospel any man has had. We can come to know Christ better by quiet meditation.

II. STUDY CONSTANTLY THE LORD'S MESSAGE.

If we are to come to know Christ intimately, we must make the most of the Bible. The entire message of the Bible centers about Christ. We must know the Bible if we would know Christ well.

III. SPEAK OFTEN WITH THE LORD.

We come to know people by talking with them and hearing them speak. So with the Lord Jesus we come to know Him by talking with Him. In prayer we speak to the Father and hear Him speak to us.

IV. SEEK FELLOWSHIP WITH OTHER CHRISTIANS.

Even though Paul did not go immediately to Jerusalem to see the apostles, he eventually did go, and had days of fellowship with Peter and James. Fellowship with consecrated and well-informed Christians may mean much to young Christians in coming to know Christ and His will and way for life.

V. SERVE THE SAVIOUR IN SINCERITY.

Jesus said, "Take my yoke upon you, and learn of me." In other words, when a Christian gets under the problems of the Saviour and serves with Him, he will come to know Him.

We will know Him when we think with Him. We will

know Him when we suffer with Him. We will see His love for the lost and desire to have the same when we serve with Him. Paul served with Christ in a matchless way.

Set your heart to know Christ better and better. In meditation, Bible study, prayer, fellowship and service, seek to know Him and the fellowship of His suffering and the power of His resurrection.

THREE POSITIONS OF THE BELIEVER

(Philippians 3)

I. FOUND IN CHRIST (vs. 9) — His Place.
II. FELLOWSHIP WITH CHRIST (vs. 10) — His Privilege.
III. FASHIONED LIKE CHRIST (vs. 21) — His Prospect.

—Five Hundred Children's Subjects
JOHN RITCHIE

THE RESOURCES OF THE CHRISTIAN

For in him dwelleth all the fulness of the Godhead bodily
(Colossians 2:9).

I. THE LORD JESUS CHRIST IS OUR PASSOVER
(I Corinthians 5:7)

II. THE LORD JESUS CHRIST IS OUR SALVATION
(Luke 2:27-30; 19:9; Isaiah 12:2; 49:6)

III. THE LORD JESUS CHRIST IS OUR LIFE
(Colossians 3:4; I John 5:12)

IV. THE LORD JESUS CHRIST IS OUR PEACE
(Ephesians 2:13, 14; Colossians 1:20)

V. THE LORD JESUS CHRIST IS OUR WISDOM, AND RIGHTEOUSNESS, AND SANCTIFICATION, AND REDEMPTION
(I Corinthians 1:30)

VI. THE LORD JESUS CHRIST IS OUR STRENGTH
(Philippians 3:13; Ephesians 6:10; Psalm 18:2)
VII. THE LORD JESUS CHRIST IS OUR VICTORY
(I Corinthians 15:57; Romans 8:37)

—Treasures of Bible Truth

LIFE IN CHRIST

(Colossians 3:1-4)

I. A RESURRECTED LIFE (verse 1a).
II. AN ELEVATING LIFE (verse 1b, 2).
III. A NEW LIFE (verse 3a).
IV. A PROTECTED LIFE (verse 3b).
V. THE CHRIST LIFE (verse 4a).
VI. A HOPEFUL LIFE (verse 4b).
VII. A FUTURE LIFE (verse 4c).

—Harlen H. Clayton

MIND NOT EARTHLY THINGS

Set your affection on things above, not on things on the earth (Colossians 3:2).

I. WORLDLY THINGS SHOULD NOT ENGROSS US
A. Because they are beneath us
B. Because they are unsuited to us
C. Because they cannot satisfy us
D. Because they are unnecessary to us
II. HEAVENLY THINGS ARE WORTHY OF OUR LOVE
A. Because they are suitable to our natures
B. Because our relations are there
C. Because our treasure is there

—Pulpit Germs

THE SERVANT IS TO —

WALK	— — — —	—I Thessalonians 4:12
WATCH	— — — —	—I Thessalonians 5:6
WAIT	— — — —	—I Thessalonions 1:10
WITNESS	— — — —	—I Thessalonians 1:7
WARN	— — — —	—I Thessalonians 5:14
WORK	— — — —	—I Thessalonians 1:3

—Pegs for Preachers

EIGHT POINTS FOR WORKERS

I. STRONG. "Be strong in the grace" —II Timothy 2:1

II. ENDURE. "Endure hardness" — —II Timothy 2:3

III. STUDY. "Study to show thy self approved"
— — — — — — — —II Timothy 2:15

IV. SHUN. "Shun profane and vain babblings"
— — — — — — — —II Timothy 2:16

V. FLEE. "Flee also youthful lusts" —II Timothy 2:22

VI. AVOID. "Foolish and unlearned questions avoid.
— — — — — — — —II Timothy 2:23

VII. PATIENT. "The servant . . . patient" II Timothy 2:24

VIII. FOLLOW. "Follow righteousness" etc. II Timothy 2:22

—Bible Themes for Busy Workers

THREEFOLD WORK OF CHRIST

(Titus 2)

I. WORK OF GRACE — verse 11 — Past

II. WORK OF GODLINESS — verse 12 — Present

III. WORK OF GLORY — verse 13 — Future

—1,000 SERMON OUTLINES
T. W. Callaway

SALVATION

(Titus 2:11)

I. EFFECTED THROUGH GRACE (II Timothy 1:9)
II. MERITED THROUGH CHRIST (Romans 4:25)
III. REVEALED THROUGH MERCY (Ephesians 2:4-5)
IV. ACCEPTED THROUGH FAITH (Hebrews 11:6)

TITLES OF CHRIST IN HEBREWS

I. SON
"His Son" — — — — — — —Chapter 1:2
II. CAPTAIN
"Captain of their salvation" — — —Chapter 2:10
III. APOSTLE
"Consider the apostle" — — — —Chapter 3:1
IV. HIGH PRIEST
"A great high priest" — — — —Chapter 4:14
V. FORERUNNER
"The forerunner is for us entered" —Chapter 6:20
VI. MEDIATOR
"The Mediator of the new testament" —Chapter 9:15
VII. AUTHOR
"The Author and Finisher of our faith" Chapter 12:2
VIII. SHEPHERD
"That great Shepherd of the sheep" —Chapter 13:20
—Bible Themes for Busy Workers

THE OLD OLD STORY

Wherefore He is able also to save them to the uttermost that come unto God by Him, seeing He ever liveth to make intercession for them (Hebrews 7:25).

I. THE GROUND OF THE COMFORT HERE OFFERED TO EVERY SINNER THAT COMES TO CHRIST: NAMELY, THAT JESUS

CHRIST EVER LIVETH TO MAKE INTERCESSION FOR SINNERS
THAT COME UNTO GOD BY HIM.

A. He is a living Saviour. He abideth for ever.

B. He dies no more, but He never ceases to plead.

C. He is a living, a sympathizing, and an active Saviour.

II. TO WHOM IS THIS COMFORT GIVEN? TO THEM THAT
COME UNTO GOD BY HIM.

A. Some do not come to God at all.

1. But all who come to Him, no matter what they
are, or may have been, may obtain salvation.

B. We come to God by repentance and prayer, but
the saving way is by faith.

III. INQUIRE MORE PARTICULARLY INTO THE COMFORT THERE
IS IN THE TEXT.

"To the uttermost." What does that mean?

A. The uttermost of human sins, whatever that uttermost sin may be.

B. The uttermost of despair.

C. The uttermost of evil habit.

D. The uttermost of temptation.

E. The uttermost of time.

—*Three Hundred Outlines on the New Testament*

THE CHRISTIAN'S RACE

(Hebrews 12:1-2)

I. THE PERSONALITIES AT THE RACE — "A cloud of witnesses"

II. THE PREPARATION FOR THE RACE — "Lay aside every weight"

III. THE PERSISTENCE IN THE RACE — "Run with patience"

IV. THE PURPOSE OF THE RACE — "Looking unto Jesus"

—*C. M. Warr*

THREE APPEARINGS OF CHRIST

(Hebrews 9:24-28)
I. HE ONCE APPEARED (verse 26) — Atonement
II. HE NOW APPEARS (verse 24) — Advocacy
III. HE SHALL APPEAR (verse 28) — Advent
—500 BIBLE SUBJECTS
John Ritchie

THINGS THAT ACCOMPANY SALVATION

(Hebrews 6:9)
I. KNOWLEDGE OF SALVATION (Luke 1:77) — By the Word
I. JOY OF SALVATION (Psalm 51:12) — In the Soul
III. STRENGTH OF SALVATION (Isaiah 33:6) — By the Spirit
VI. HOPE OF SALVATION (I Thessalonians 5:8) — At the Advent   —*John Ritchie*

WHAT CHRISTIANS SHOULD BE

Well pleasing in his sight (Hebrews 13:21).
I. IMITATORS OF GOD —Ephesians 5:1
II. BLAMELESS — — —Ephesians 1:4; I Peter 1:14-16
III. TRANSFORMED — —Romans 12:2
IV. SEPARATED — — —II Corinthians 6:17
V. EXAMPLES — — —I Timothy 4:12
VI. FRUITFUL — — —Romans 7:4
VII. THANKFUL — — —Colossians 3:15; Ephesians 5:20
VIII. CONTENTED — — —Hebrews 13:5
—TREASURES OF BIBLE TRUTH
William H. Schweinfurth

FOUR ASPECTS OF SALVATION

(I Peter 1:1-5)
I. ELECT BY THE WILL OF THE FATHER (verse 2).

II. Sheltered by the Blood of Christ (verse 2).
III. Begotten by the Resurrection of Christ (verse 3).
IV. Kept by the Power of God (verse 5).

—500 Scripture Outlines
John Ritchie

GOD'S PEOPLE

But ye are a peculiar people (I Peter 2:9).

I. God's People Are a Professing People
II. God's People Are a Separated People
III. God's People Are a Suffering People
IV. God's People Are a Praying People
V. God's People Are a Sanctified People
VI. God's People Are a Blessed People

—Pulpit Germs
W. W. Wythe

"LIVE IT DOWN"

Having your conversation honest among the Gentiles; that whereas they speak against you as evil-doers, they may by your good works, which they behold, glorify God in the day of visitation (I Peter 2:12).

I. The World's Treatment of Christians
   A. Enmity
   B. Defamation
   C. Perversion of the truth
   D. Aggravation of circumstances
II. The Behavior Recommended
   A. Honesty
   B. Consistency
   C. Truthfulness
   D. Purity
   E. Fidelity

   F. Circumspection
  III. THE RESULTS THAT WILL OBTAIN
    A. God will be glorified
    B. His religion will be honored
    C. Men will be saved

          —Pulpit Germs

GROWTH IN GRACE

Grow in grace (II Peter 3:18).

 I. FALSE MARKS OF GROWTH IN GRACE
  A. Increasing religious knowledge.
  B. Pleasure in conversing on religious topics.
  C. Pleasure in hearing the Word.
  D. Zeal for the cause of religion.
 II. THE TRUE MARKS OF GROWTH IN GRACE
  A. An increasing humility.
  B. A self-denying spirit.
  C. Simplicity and ingenuousness of mind.
  D. Increasing hatred of falsehood and artifice.
 III. THE MEANS TO BE USED
  A. Secret prayer.
  B. A diligent perusal of the Word.
  C. Careful self-examination.

       —THE PULPIT SYNOPSIS
        Richard Cope

THREEFOLD LOVE OF GOD

(I John 3:1)

 I. MANNER — "Behold, what manner"
 II. MEANING — "Called the sons of God"
 III. MEASURE — "World knoweth us not"

     —1,000 SERMON OUTLINES
      T. W. Callaway

PRECIOUS P'S

(I John 3:1-3)
I. PRICELESS PRIVILEGE (verse 1)
II. POSITIVE PROMISE (verse 2)
III. PURIFYING POWER (verse 3)
—*Gleanings*

THE VICTOR'S CROWN

I will give thee a crown of life (Revelation 2:10).
I. THE CHRISTIAN'S REWARD IS GLORIOUS—"A crown"
II. THE CHRISTIAN'S REWARD IS DURABLE—"A crown of life"
III. THE CHRISTIAN'S REWARD IS PERSONAL—"I will give Thee"
—*Pulpit Germs*

THE SEVEN CHURCHES

A HISTORY OF THE ENTIRE CHURCH THROUGH THE AGES
Revelation 2, 3
EPHESUS, the Church in Early Purity
SMYRNA, the Church in Persecution
PERGAMOS, the Church united with the World
THYATIRA, Romanism Ruling Supreme
SARDIS, Protestantism
PHILADELPHIA, the Faithful Few
LAODICEA, the World-Church
The last four go on together until the end.
500 *Bible Subjects*

A GRACIOUS INVITATION

And whosoever will, let him take the water of life freely (Revelation 22:17).
The Bible not only makes known our wants, but tells

us where they may be supplied. Without water our bodies perish. Without the Living Water our souls are consumed with thirst. All man's spiritual needs are met and satisfied by Christ.

I. THE BLESSING — "Water"

Water is cleansing. Christ cleanses from sin.

Water is satisfying. Christ meets our yearning after God.

Water is beautifying and fertilizing. Christ makes us holy, beautiful, useful.

II. THE CHARACTERS INVITED:

The thirsty, "Blessed are they which do hunger and thirst after righteousness."

The whole of the race, "Whosoever will." If any go athirst, it is not for want of an invitation, but because they will not drink of the Water of Life.

III. THE AGENCY EMPLOYED:

The Spirit. The Holy Spirit is continually pressing home this invitation

The Bride — the Church. Not any particular section or sect, but the Universal Church of Christ. "All who love and serve the Lord Jesus."

This soul-satisfying Water of Life is the free gift of God. It is an inexhaustible Fountain, which can never fail.

Obey the invitation. Drink, and thy thrist shall be eternally quenched, the soul eternally satisfied.

—*Sermons in a Nutshell*

Miscellaneous

THE BELIEVER

HIS SALVATION — — — — — (Hebrews 5:9)
HIS PRESERVATION — — — — (Jude 1)

HIS PRESENTATION — — — — (Romans 12:1)
HIS PROCLAMATION — — — — (II Timothy 4:2)
HIS EXCLAMATION — — — — (Zechariah 9:17)
HIS OCCUPATION — — — — (I Peter 2:16)
HIS CONSUMATION — — — — (John 17:24)

—Pegs for Preachers

ATTITUDE OF THE BELIEVER

LOOKING — — — — (Hebrews 12:2)
LISTENING — — — — (Psalm 85:8)
LEARNING — — — — (Matthew 11:29)
LIVING — — — — — (Philippians 1:21)
LYING — — — — — (Psalm 23:2)
LOVING — — — — — (I John 4:19)
LONGING — — — — (Psalm 119:174)

—Pegs for Preachers

THE BELIEVER'S CALLING

I. He who calls — God — — — — (Romans 8:28-30)
II. From what He calls — darkness — (I Peter 2:9)

Sonship— — (I John 3:1)
Saints — — (Romans 1:7)
Servants — (I Peter 2:16)

III. To what He calls us   Unity — — (Col. 3:15)
Fellowship — (I Cor. 1:9)
Suffering — (I Peter 2:21)
Kingdom — (I Thess. 2:12)

IV. Character of the calling Holy — — (II Tim. 1:9)
Heavenly — (Heb. 3:1)

—Pegs for Preachers

BURDENS

Every man shall bear his own burden (Galatians 6:5).
Bear ye one another's burdens (Galatians 6:2).
Cast thy burden on the Lord (Psalm 25:22).

There is a threefold cord not easily broken. There is no contradiction, not the slightest discordance in these texts.

I. God Has Ordained That Every One Shall Bear a Burden.

    A. Some burdens are inseparable; deliverance from them is impossible.

        1. The burden of sorrow visits alike the palace and the hut.

           a. Every man must bear that burden.

        2. Our responsibilities, our physical infirmities, the difficulties of work, we all must bear them.

           a. No one can carry them for us.

II. There Are Loads We Can Help Others to Carry, and Thus Learn Sympathy.

    A. There is a sense in which we can bear each other's burdens and trials.

        1. No man is beyond the reach of human sympathy.

        2. Often a light lift, a mere touch, helps us over sorrow marvellously.

    B. If we get faint with discouragement, let us take hold of Christ and He will help us to carry our burden.

III. The Third Text Takes Us From Self-Help and Brotherly Help Up to the Divine Help.

    A. God does not release us from performance of duty, but He will sustain us in doing it.

    B. The load will not crush us, God's love will carry us and our burden too.

C. The most overwhelming burden in God's universe
is sin!

1. Jesus Christ bore that burden for us.

—*Three Hundred Outlines on the New Testament*

THE CHILD OF GOD SHOULD BE STEADFAST

IN FAITH — — — —(I Peter 5:9)
IN WORK — — — —(I Corinthians 15:58)
IN LOOKING — — —(Acts 1:10)
IN DOCTRINE — — —(Acts 2:42)
IN MIND — — — —(Ruth 1:18)

—*Pegs for Preachers*

WHAT A CHILD OF GOD SHOULD HAVE

Christ in his heart — — — — (Colossians 1:27)
Glory in his face — — — — (Acts 6:15)
The Spirit as his teacher — — (John 14:26)
Fear of God to guide him — — (Proverbs 8:13)
Path of holiness to walk in — — (Isaiah 35:11)
Heaven as his destination — — (John 14:2)

—*Pegs for Preachers*

YE BELONG TO CHRIST

I. "Ye are not your own, for ye are bought with a price"
(I Cor. 6:20)

A. His purchased possession — — (Eph. 1:14)

B. His redeemed — — — — (I Peter 18:19)

C. His peculiar treasure — — — (Mal. 3:17, R.V.)

D. His temple, of which He is the
chief cornerstone — — — — (Eph. 2:20-22)

   E. His Church, of which He is the
      Head — — — — — — (Eph. 5:23)
II. Members of His body, and of His flesh and of His bones
                          (Eph. 5:30)
III. Quickened together with him; raised up together
    with Him; sealed together with Him
                       (Eph. 2:5, 6)

IV. "Because Ye Belong to Christ"
   A. "Beloved . . . be diligent, that
     ye may be found in Him in
     peace, without spot, and blame-
     less — — — — — — — (II Peter 3:14)
                    —Twelve Baskets Full

WHAT CHRIST IS

    I. He is *"the Truth"*
       (John 14:6)   Let us *believe* Him

   II. He is *"the True Bread"*
       (John 6:32)   Let us *feast* upon Him

 III. He is *"the True Vine"*
       (John 15:1)   Let us *abide* in Him

  IV. He is *"the Holy and*   Let us be *holy* and *true*
     the True" (Rev. 3:7)   with Him

   V. He is *"the True Wit-*
     ness" (Rev. 3:14)   Let us *listen* to Him

  VI. He is *"the True Light"* Let us be *illuminated* by
     (John 1:9)   Him

 VII. He is *"the True God"*
     (I John 1:20)   Let us *adore* Him
     A. As "the Truth"   He delivers us from error
     B. As "the True   He makes us independent of
       Bread"   earth's joy

C. As "the True Vine"	He enables us to give joy to the Father who is seeking fruit
D. As "the True Witness"	He would restore our souls when we get into Laodicean lukewarmness
E. As "the Holy and the True"	He is the Pattern of what the church should be
F. As "the True Light"	The Pillar of Fire to guide us through the darkness of this world
G. As "the True God"	He is to receive equal honor with the Father, the Object of worship

—Twelve Baskets Full

WHAT CHRIST DOES FOR HIS PEOPLE

He Quickens Them (John 5:25) —	—As the Life Giver
He Saves Them (Matthew 1:21)—	—As the Saviour
He Seals Them (Ephesians 1:13)	—As the Owner
He Leads Them (John 10:27) —	—As the Shepherd
He Succours Them (Hebrews 2)—	—As the Priest
He Restores Them (I John 2:1)—	—As the Advocate
He Comes for Them (John 14:3)	—As the Bridegroom

—500 Bible Subjects

THE DEITY OF CHRIST

PROCLAIMED BY THE FATHER (Matthew 1:23; John 1:1)
CLAIMED BY THE SON (John 10:30; 5:21; Revelation 1:8)
WITNESSED BY THE SPIRIT (Hebrews 1:8; I Peter 3:15 R.V.)

OWNED BY ANGELS (Hebrews 1:6; Revelation 5:11-12)
CONFESSED BY SAINTS (John 20:28; Romans 9:5)
FEARED BY DEMONS (Mark 5:7; James 2:19)
MANIFESTED BY HIS WORKS (Luke 7:20; John 5:36)
—500 *Bible Subjects*

THE CHRISTIAN'S RELATION TO THE WORLD

BORN INTO THE WORLD (John 16:21)
GIVEN OUT OF THE WORLD (John 17:6)
DELIVERED FROM THE WORLD (Galatians 1:4)
CRUCIFIED TO THE WORLD (Galatians 6:14)
NOT OF THE WORLD (John 17:16)
A STRANGER IN THE WORLD (I John 3:2)
HATED BY THE WORLD (John 17:14)
—500 *Bible Subjects*

THE CHRISTIAN'S PLACE IN THE WORLD

SENT INTO THE WORLD (John 17:18; 20:21)
PREACHING TO THE WORLD (Mark 15:15)
THE LIGHT OF THE WORLD (Philippians 2:15; Matthew 5:14)
LIVE GODLY IN THE WORLD (Titus 2:12)
NOT CONFORMED TO THE WORLD (Romans 12:2; John 17:15)
LOVE NOT THE WORLD (I John 2:16; II Timothy 4:10)
PASSING THROUGH THE WORLD (I Peter 2:11)
NO FRIENDSHIP WITH THE WORLD (James 4:4; 1:27)
—500 *Bible Subjects*

SEVEN MARKS OF A CHRISTIAN

I. A Christian is a man who is BORN AGAIN: "Born again, not of corruptible seed, but of incorruptible,

by the word of God, which liveth and abideth forever" (I Peter 1:23).

II. A Christian is a man who doesn't seek for SALVATION
THROUGH WORKS: "Not of works, lest any man should
boast" (Ephesians 2:9); "God imputeth righteousness
without works" (Romans 4:6).

III. A Christian is a man who shows by his works that
he has got SALVATION THROUGH CHRIST: "Who gave
Himself for us, that He might redeem us from all
iniquity, and purify unto Himself a peculiar people,
zealous of good works" (Titus 2:14).

IV. A Christian is a man who BUILDS ON A SURE FOUNDA-
TION: "Other foundation can no man lay than that
is laid, which is Jesus Christ" (I Corinthians 3:11).

V. A Christian is a man who CONFESSES CHRIST among
his fellows: "With the mouth confession is made unto
salvation" (Romans 10:10).

VI. A Christian is a man who SERVES THE LORD JESUS
AND WAITS FOR HIS COMING: He has "turned to God
from idols to serve the living God, and to wait for
His Son from Heaven" (I Thessalonians 1:9,10).

VII. A Christian is a man who CARRIES THE MESSAGE OF
SALVATION to others and beseeches men, saying: "We
pray you in Christ's stead be ye reconciled to God"
(II Corinthians 5:20).

—1,000 SUBJECTS FOR SPEAKERS
AND STUDENTS

SEVEN THINGS CHRISTIANS SHOULD DO

They should live —

I. A LIFE OF HOLINESS (I Thess. 5:22; II Timothy 2:19).

II. A LIFE OF PRAYER (I Tim. 2:8; I Thess. 5:17).

III. A LIFE OF DEATH (Heb. 11:6; Col. 1:23).

IV. A LIFE OF SELF-DENIAL (Matt. 5:29; Gal. 5:24).

 V. A LIFE OF SEPARATION FROM WORLD (Exodus 32:26).

VI. A LIFE OF CONSECRATION (Exod. 28:40-41; Rom. 12:1).

VII. A LIFE OF SERVICE (Deut. 10:12; Luke 16:13).

—Seed Basket

CONVERSION

A New Attitude toward God, an Outward Change in the Life

THE ACT (I Thess. 1:9; I Peter 2:24; Acts 26:18)

THE NEED (Matt. 18:3; Acts 3:19; Isa. 53:6)

THE MOTIVE (Acts 11:21; Hosea 14:8; Phil. 3:8)

THE HINDRANCES (Acts 28:27; 13:8; John 6:66)

—500 Bible Subjects

REASONS FOR NOT FEARING

He REDEEMS me — — — —Isaiah 43:1

He PROTECTS me — — — —Genesis 15:1

He STRENGTHENS me — — —Isaiah 35:4

He is WITH me — — — —Isaiah 41:10

He HELPS me — — — — —Isaiah 41:13

He CARES for me — — — —Matthew 10:31

He has a KINGDOM for me — —Luke 12:32

—Pegs for Preachers

THE BELIEVER'S FEET

SET ON A ROCK (Psalm 40:2)—Salvation

CLEANSED BY THE WORD (John 13:10)—Communion

KEPT BY DIVINE POWER (I Samuel 2:9)—Preservation

SHOD WITH PEACE (Ephesians 6:15)—Warfare

RUNNING WITH THE GOSPEL (Romans 10:15)—Service
BRUISING SATAN (Romans 16:20)—Victory
—500 Bible Subjects

THE FEET BY NATURE

I.	ALMOST GONE — — — —	(Psalm 73:2)
II.	RUNNING TO EVIL — — —	(Proverbs 1:16)
III.	RUNNING TO MISCHIEF — —	(Proverbs 6:18)
IV.	ON THE DARK MOUNTAINS —	(Jeremiah 13:16)
V.	SUNK IN THE MIRE — — —	(Jeremiah 38:22)
VI.	SWIFT TO SHED BLOOD — —	(Romans 3:15)
VII.	SLIDE IN DUE TIME— — —	(Deuteronomy 32:35)

THE FEET BY GRACE

I.	WASHED — — — — —	(John 13:10)
II.	KEPT — — — — — —	(I Samuel 2:9)
III.	SET UPON A ROCK — — —	(Psalm 40:2)
IV.	NOT TO BE MOVED — — —	(Psalm 66:9)
V.	SHOD WITH THE GOSPEL — —	(Ephesians 6:15)
VI.	BRINGING THE GOSPEL — —	(Romans 10:15)
VII.	BRUISING SATAN — — —	(Romans 16:20)

—Twelve Baskets Full

THE DEVELOPMENT OF FAITH

I.	NO FAITH— — — — —	(Mark 4:40)
II.	LITTLE FAITH — — — —	(Luke 12:28)
III.	GREAT FAITH — — — —	(Matthew 8:10)
IV.	RICH FAITH — — — —	(James 2:5)
V.	PRECIOUS FAITH — — —	(II Peter 1:1)

VI. Full Faith — — — — (Acts 6:5)
VII. Perfect Faith — — — (James 2:22)
—*Twelve Baskets Full*

GOD'S PURPOSE IN CHASTENING

For Proving — — — — (Deuteronomy 8:2-3)
For Purifying — — — (Malachi 3:3)
For Teaching — — — — (Psalm 119:71)
For Humbling — — — (II Corinthians 12:7)
For Restoring — — — (Psalm 119:67)
For Promotion — — — (Daniel 3:23, 30)
—*Pegs for Preachers*

A SEVENFOLD VIEW OF THE LOVE OF GOD

It is Infinite — —in its character — (John 17:23)
It is Constraining —in its power — — (II Cor. 5:14)
It is Inseparable —in its object — — (Rom. 8:35-37)
It is Individual —in its choice — — (Galatians 2:20)
It is Universal —in its extent — — (John 3:16)
It is Unchanging —in its purpose — (John 8:1)
It is Everlasting —in its duration — (Jeremiah 31:3)
—*Peg for Preachers*

GOD'S WORD

I. What It Does for Me
   A. Quickens me. "Quicken thou me according to Thy Word." (Psalm 119:25)
   B. Sanctifies me. "Sanctify them through thy truth." (John 17:17)

    C. CLEANSES me. "Wherewithal . . according to Thy Word." (Psalm 119:9)

II. WHAT IT IS TO ME
    A. PRECIOUS "The word . . . was precious in those days." (I Samuel 3:1)
    B. PENETRATING "Piercing even . . . soul and spirit." (Hebrews 4:12)
    C. POWERFUL "Like a hammer." (Jeremiah 23:29)
    D. PURIFYING "Like as a fire." (Jeremiah 23:29)
    E. PROTECTING "Sword of the spirit." (Ephesians 6:17)

III. HOW IT SHOULD BE TREATED BY ME
    I am to —
    A. LOVE it "How love I thy law!" (Psalm 119:97)
    B. SEARCH it "Search the Scriptures." (John 5:39)
    C. FEED ON it "I did eat them." (Thy Words) (Jeremiah 15:16)
    D. HOLD FAST to it "Holding fast the faithful word." (Titus 1:9)
    E. PREACH it "Preach the word." (II Timothy 4:2)
    F. MEDITATE ON it "I will meditate on Thy precepts." (Psalm 119:15)
    G. DELIGHT IN it "I will delight in Thy statutes." (Psalm 119:16)

        —Bible Themes for Busy Workers

SEVEN CHARACTERISTICS OF THE PEOPLE OF GOD

I. CHARACTERISTICS
    A. DISCIPLES—In the same school—One Master—Acts 20:7
    B. CHILDREN—In the same family—One Father
                        —John 11:52
    C. SHEEP—In the same flock—One Shepherd
                        —John 10:16

D. Saints—In the same covenant—One rank
—Romans 1:7

E. Stones—In the same house—One foundation
—I Peter 2:5

F. Members—In the same body—One Head
—Romans 12:5

G. The Bride—In the same glory—One Bridegroom
Revelation 21:2, 9

II. Application

A. All believers are alike disciples, though some have not made the same progress as others.

B. All are alike children, sharing the same life, though some of them are mere babes, others young men or fathers in growth.

C. All are alike sheep, though some follow the Shepherd more closely, listening to His voice.

D. All are alike saints by calling, though some are more practically holy in their walk and conversation than others.

E. All are alike living stones upon the one foundation, though some are more prominent in the building than others.

F. All are alike members of the body, though some have a more honorable place and office than others.

G. All will be together in the same glory, though some will suffer loss through unfaithfulness when in the body.

—Twelve Baskets Full

WORKING FOR GOD

Exhortation for the work "Go" — — (Matthew 21:28)
Sphere for the work "My Vineyard" — (Matthew 21:28)
Season for the work "To-day" — — (Matthew 21:28)

POWER for the work "Holy Ghost" — — (Acts 1:8)
RESULT of the work "Added" etc. — — (Acts 2:41)
REWARD for the work "Shall shine" — — (Daniel 12:3)
—*Pegs for Preachers*

THREE EXAMPLES OF DEALING WITH GOD

WAITING ON GOD (Psalm 130:5) — David
WALKING WITH GOD (Genesis 5:22) — Enoch
WORKING FOR GOD (Hebrews 11:7) — Noah
—500 *Scripture Outlines*

THE HOLY SPIRIT

I. WHAT HE IS
   A. He is a Person. "Descended in bodily shape."
      (Luke 3:22)
   B. He Always Existed. "The eternal Spirit." (Hebrews
      9:14)
   C. He is Omniscient. "Searcheth all things." (I Cor-
      inthians 2:10)
   D. He is Omnipresent. "Whither shall I go," etc.
      (Psalm 139:7-11)
   E. He is Omnipotent. Raised the dead witnesses.
      (Revelation 11:11)
II. HIS OPERATIONS
   A. Convinces. "Convince the world of sin." (Mar.)
      (John 16:8)
   B. Quickens. "Quicken . . . by His Spirit." (Romans
      8:11)
   C. Indwells. "If the spirit . . . dwell in you." (Ro-
      mans 8:9)
   D. Comforts. "Another Comforter." John 14:16-17)

E. Seals. "Sealed with that Holy Spirit." (Ephesians 1:13)

F. Reveals. "Revealed . . . by the Spirit." (Ephesians 3:5)

G. Sanctifies. "Sanctified . . . by the Spirit." (I Corinthians 6:11)

H. Leads. "Led by the Spirit of God." (Romans 8:14)

I. Witnesses. "The Spirit itself beareth witness." (Romans 8:16)

—Bible Themes for Busy Workers

TRUTHS CONNECTED WITH THE HOLY SPIRIT

I. THE HOLY SPIRIT

   A. Convicts the World — — (John 16:8-12)

   B. Regenerates the Believing
one   — — — — — (John 3:5-7; I John 5:7)

   C. Indwells the Child of God (John 14:17)

   D. Seals the Saint — — — (Ephesians 1:13)

   E. Is the Comforter and
Guide — — — — — (John 15:26; 16:13)

   F. Is the Unction or Holy
Anointing — — — — (I John 2:20)

   G. Is the Earnest of Coming
Glory — — — — — (Ephesians 1:14)

II. THE CHRISTIAN IS EXHORTED TO

   A. Be Filled with the Spirit (Ephesians 5:18)

   B. Pray in the Spirit — — (Jude 20; Eph. 6:18)

   C. Sing in the Spirit — — (Ephesians 5:19)

   D. Worship in the Spirit — (John 4:23; Phil. 3:3)

   E. Walk in the Spirit — — (Galatians 5:16)

   F. Be Led by the Spirit — (Galatians 5:18)

G. Remember His Body is the Temple of the Holy
   Spirit — — — — — (I Corinthians 6:19)
                              —*Twelve Baskets Full*

THE TOUCH OF JESUS —

ITS POWER PHYSICALLY AND SPIRITUALLY

GIVES LIFE — (Mark 5:41; John 11:25, 26; Ephesians 2:5)

CLEANSES THE FOULEST — (Matthew 8:3; I Corinthians 6:11;
   Ephesians 5:27)

HEALS THE FEVER-STRICKEN — (Matthew 8:15; John 14:27;
   Hebrews 4:3)

OPENS BLIND EYES — (Matthew 9:29; Mark 8:22-25; John
   8:12)

MAKES DUMB LIPS SPEAK — (Mark 7:32-35; Isaiah 35:6; Acts
   2:4; Acts 19:6)

CLEANSES LONG-STANDING SECRET DISEASE — (Matthew 9:20;
   Psalm 19:12; Exodus 15:26)

HEALS PERFECTLY — (Matthew 14:36; Acts 3:16)

HEALS WOUNDS CAUSED BY DISCIPLES — (Luke 22:51; Luke
   23:34)

BANISHES FEAR — (Matthew 27:7; John 14:1; Hebrews 13:6)

STAYS SORROW — (Luke 7:13-14; Psalm 58:12; John 14:27)

WELCOMES LITTLE ONES — Mark 10:13-16; Matthew 18:2-5)

MEETS EVERY NEED — (Luke 6:19; II Corinthians 7:9)
                              —*Sermons in a Nutshell*

TWO MIGHTY INTERCESSORS

I. We have an Advocate with the Father — Jesus Christ the Righteous. (I John 2:1)
   He ever liveth to make intercession
   for us. .... (Hebrews 7:25)

II. The Spirit Himself maketh intercession for us, with groanings
which cannot be uttered: He maketh intercession for the saints ac-
cording to the will of God. .... (Romans 8:26, 27)
—Twelve Baskets Full

DOUBLE TITLES GIVEN TO THE LORD JESUS

I. THE AUTHOR AND FINISHER of Our
Faith— — — — — — — — (Hebrews 12:2)
II. THE APOSTLE AND HIGH PRIEST of Our
Profession — — — — — — (Hebrews 3:1)
III. THE SHEPHERD AND BISHOP of Our
Souls— — — — — — — — (I Peter 2:25)
—Twelve Baskets Full

JOSEPH AND JESUS

I. Joseph, the SHEPHERD — — —(Genesis 49:24)
Joseph, STRIPPED — — — —(Genesis 37:23)
Joseph, SOLD — — — — —(Genesis 37:28)
Joseph, IN THE PIT — — — —(Genesis 37:24)
Joseph, FALSLEY ACCUSED — —(Genesis 39:14)
Joseph, IN PRISON — — — —(Genesis 39:20)
Joseph, HATED — — — — —(Genesis 37:4)
Joseph, WEPT — — — — —(Genesis 50:17)
Joseph, RAISED to the highest place
in Egypt — — — — — —(Genesis 41:40)
II. Jesus, the GOOD SHEPHERD — —(John 10:11)
Jesus, STRIPPED — — — — —(Matthew 27:28)
Jesus, SOLD — — — — —(Matthew 26:15)

Jesus, IN THE PIT — — — — (Psalm 88:4)
Jesus, FALSELY ACCUSED — — — (Mark 14:56-57)
Jesus, IN PRISON   — — — — (Isaiah 53:8)
Jesus, HATED   — — — — — (John 15:24)
Jesus, WEPT   — — — — — (John 11:35)
Jesus RAISED to the highest place
  in Glory — — — — — — (Ephesians 1:20-21)
                          —*Pegs for Preachers*

JUDGMENT

In Various Aspects

JUDGMENT OF THE SINNER, Predicted (Hebrews 9:27; Ecclesiastes 11:9; II Peter 2:2-4; Hebrews 10:27)

JUDGMENT OF THE BELIEVER, Past (John 5:24 R.V.; Romans 8:1; 8:23-24; Galatians 2:20)

JUDGMENT OF THE SERVANT, Future (II Corinthians 5:10; Revelation 22:12; Colossians 3:24-25; I Corinthians 4:1-5)

                          —500 *Bible Subjects*

JUSTIFICATION

A New State before God, a Forensic Term

THE SINNER'S STATE (Romans 3:10; Isaiah 64:6; Romans 3:9)

GOD, THE JUSTIFIER (Romans 8:33; 4:25)

CHRIST'S DEATH THE PROCURING CAUSE (I Peter 3:18)

GRACE THE SPRING (Romans 3:24; Galatians 2:16-24)

FAITH THE PRINCIPLE (Romans 5:1; Acts 13:39)

RESURRECTION THE WITNESS (Romans 4:25; 5:18)

WORKS THE EVIDENCE (James 2:26; Titus 3:8)

                          —500 *Bible Subjects*

OUR HOPE

I. THE COMING OF THE LORD IS —

A. A saving hope — — — — (Romans 8:24)
B. A good hope — — — — — (II Thessalonians 2:16)
C. A blessed hope — — — — (Titus 2:13)
D. A joyful hope — — — — (Hebrews 3:6)
E. A living hope — — — — (I Peter 1:3)
F. A purifying hope — — — — (I John 3:3)
G. A hope of righteousness — — (Galatians 5:5)

—Twelve Baskets Full

THE LIPS

THE LIPS BY NATURE

I. Unclean— — — — — — — (Isaiah 6:5)
II. Uncircumcised — — — — — (Exodus 6:12)
III. Flattering — — — — — — (Psalm 12:2, 3)
IV. Lying — — — — — — — (Proverbs 12:22)
V. Dissembling— — — — — — (Proverbs 26:24)
VI. Contentious — — — — — — (Proverbs 18:6)
VII. Holding the Poison of Asps — — (Romans 3:13)

THE LIPS BY GRACE

I. Opened — — — — — — — (Psalm 51:15)
II. Sinning Not — — — — — — (Job 2:10)
III. Joyful — — — — — — — (Psalm 63:5)
IV. Praising— — — — — — — (Psalm 119:17)
V. Keeping Knowledge — — — — (Proverbs 1:2)
VI. Dispersing Knowledge — — — (Proverbs 15:7)
VII. Giving Thanks — — — — — (Hebrews 13:15)

—Twelve Baskets Full

THE LORD OUR KEEPER

I. WHAT HE KEEPS
  A. The SPIRIT The thoughts
  B. The SOUL   The desires   (I Thessalonians 5:23)
  C. The BODY   The actions
  D. The LIPS   "Keep the door
                of my lips" (Psalm 141:3)
  E. The FEET   "He will keep
                the feet of
                His saints" (I Samuel 2:9)

II. FROM WHAT HE KEEPS
  A. From TROUBLE — — — (Psalm 32:7)
  B. From THE EVIL — — — (John 17:15)
  C. From STRIFE OF TONGUES — (Psalm 31:20)
  D. From DANGER — — — (Psalm 91:4)
  E. From STUMBLING — — — (Jude 24)

III. HOW HE KEEPS
  A. By the IMMUTABILITY OF
     GOD — — — — — — (Malachi 3:6)
  B. By the POWER — — — (I Peter 1:5)
  C. By the FAITHFULNESS — — (II Thesalonians 3:3)
  D. By the MERCY — — — (Psalm 138:8)
  E. By the LOVE — — — — (Jeremiah 31:3)
  F. By the WORD — — — — (Proverbs 6:22)
         —Bible Themes for Busy Workers

THE LORD MY PORTION

I. MY SAVIOUR— — — (Matt. 1:21; I Tim. 1:15;
               Isa. 43:11)
II. MY SUBSTITUTE — — (Isa. 53:5; II Cor. 5:21;
               Rom. 5:8)
III. MY RIGHTEOUSNESS — (Jer. 23:6; Rom. 10:4; Isa.
               54:17)

IV. My SANCTIFICATION — (I Cor.1; 2:30; Heb. 10:10)
V. My EXAMPLE   — — (Matt. 11:29; I Peter 2:21-23)
VI. My TEACHER—   — — (Matthew 17:5; Isaiah 50:4)
VII. My HIGH PRIEST — — (Hebrews 4:15; 7:26)
VIII. My LORD AND MASTER (Matt. 23:10; John 13:13, 14)
IX. My BROTHER—   — — (Rom. 8:29; Heb. 2:11, 12)
X. My FRIEND —   — — (Prov. 18:24; S. of Sol. 5:16;
    John 15:14)
XI. My KEEPER —   — — (Ps. 121:5; John 17:12;
    I Peter 1:5)
XII. My WISDOM—   — — (Prov. 3:13; 8:5; I Cor. 1:30)
XIII. My SHEPHERD   — — (Ps. 23:1; Ezek. 34:23;
    John 10:11)
XIV. My PEACE —   — — (Isa. 26:3; John 14:27;
    Eph. 2:14)
XV. My ALL IN ALL —   — (Colossians 1:19; 2:10; 3:11)
    —*Twelve Baskets Full*

PICTURE OF A RIGHTEOUS MAN

The WAY — — – of the Righteous – (Psalm 1:6)
The INHERITANCE   – of the Righteous – (Psalm 37:29)
The GLADNESS —   – of the Righteous – (Psalm 64:10)
The FLOURISHING   – of the Righteous – (Psalm 92:12)
The REMEMBRANCE – of the Righteous – (Psalm 112:6)
The THANKSGIVING – of the Righteous – (Psalm 140:13)
The SAFETY—   — – of the Righteous – (Proverbs 18:10)
The RECOMPENSE   – of the Righteous – (Proverbs 11:21)
    —*Pegs for Preachers*

NOTHING — ANYTHING — EVERYTHING

I. NOTHING
   A. With God nothing shall be
      impossible   — — — — — (Luke 1:37)

  B. Without Me ye can do nothing — (John 15:5)
  C. In nothing be anxious — — — (Phil. 4:6 R.V.)
  D. Lacked nothing — — — (Luke 22:35)
II. ANYTHING
  A. If ye shall ask anything — — (John 14:14)
  B. He shall receive anything — — (James 1:7)
  C. Is anything too hard for the
    Lord? — — — — — — (Genesis 18:14)
  D. Lacked ye anything? — — — (Luke 22:35)
III. EVERYTHING
  A. In everything by prayer — — (Philippians 4:6)
  B. In everything give thanks — — (I Thess. 1:18)
  C. I know that Thou canst do
    everything — — — — (Job 42:2)
  D. Let everything . . . Praise the
    Lord — — — — — — — (Psalm 150:6)
        —*Twelve Baskets Full*

THE LORD'S PEOPLE

Are described in the Word as
 I. A CHOSEN PEOPLE (Deuteronomy 7:6; 2:9)
 II. A REDEEMED PEOPLE (Exodus 15:13; Ephesians 1:7)
 III. A PECULIAR PEOPLE (Deuteronomy 14:2; Titus 2:14)
 IV. A SEPARATED PEOPLE (Exodus 33:16; John 15:19)
 V. A HOLY PEOPLE (Deuteronomy 7:6; I Peter 1:15)
 VI. A HAPPY PEOPLE (Deuteronomy 33:29; John 15:11)
      —*500 Bible Subjects*

SAINTS IN WRONG PLACES

 I. A DISCOURAGED WORKER
    Elijah under a juniper tree — (I Kings 19:4)

II. A Backsliding Believer
    Abraham in Egypt — — — (Genesis 12:10)
III. A Disobedient Servant
    Jonah in the sea-monster — — (Jonah 2)
IV. A Seduced Prophet
    The man of God in the old
    prophet's house — — — — (I Kings 13:19)
V. A Lazy Saint
    David on the house-top — — (II Samuel 11:2)
VI. A Silenced Witness
    Lot in Sodom — — — — (Genesis 14:12)
VII. A Miserable Disciple
    Peter before the fire — — — (Luke 22:65)
                —*Twelve Baskets Full*

SALVATION

Threefold — Past, Present, Future

Past — From Sin's Penalty (Romans 1:16; Acts 28:18; Acts 16:31; Romans 10:10; I Corinthians 15:2; II Timothy 1:9)

Present — From Sin's Power (Hebrews 7:25; Romans 5:9; James 1:23; I Timothy 4:6; Philippians 2:12)

Future — From Sin's Presence (Romans 13:11; Hebrews 9:28; Philippians 3:20; I Thessalonians 5:8)

The First is immediate, Secured by Christ's Death
The Second is continuous by Christ's Life
The Third is prospective at Christ's Coming

                —500 *Bible Subjects*

SANCTIFICATION

The word means "to set apart" or "to separate"
The Sanctification of Believers (I Corinthians 1:2; II Thessalonians 2:13; I Peter 1:3)

I. PERFECT and ONCE for All — The Work of the Cross, the Result of the Sacrifice of Christ (I Corinthians 6: 11; Acts 20:32; 26:18; Hebrews 2:11)

II. PROGRESSIVE and CONTINUOUS — The Work of the Spirit through the Word in the believer (I Thessalonians 5:23; John 17:17)

Types and Illustrations — The Sabbath sanctified (Genesis 2:3); The First-Born "set apart" (Exodus 13:2); The Brazen Altar, the Holy Garments (Exodus 29:44; 28:2) and the Holy Mount (II Peter 1:18) accounted "sacred" or "holy," not intrinsically, but "set apart" by the presence and for the service of God.   —500 *Bible Subjects*

REDEMPTION

The word means "to buy back" and set free. There is a Redemption by Blood and by Power.

MAN'S RUIN (Isaiah 52:3; John 8:34; Romans 6:20)

MAN'S HELPLESSNESS (Psalm 49:7; Micah 6:7)

A REDEEMER PROVIDED (Job 33:24; Psalm 111:9)

REDEMPTION BY BLOOD (Ephesians 1:7; Acts 20:28; Hebrews 9:12)

REDEMPTION BY POWER (Ephesians 1:13-44; 4:30; Romans 8:23)

REDEMPTION FROM INIQUITY (Titus 2:14; I Peter 1:18)

REDEMPTION FROM THE CURSE (Galatians 3:13; Psalm 103:4)

REDEMPTION OF BODY (Romans 8:23; Philippians 3:20 R.V.)
                                    —500 *Bible Subjects*

REGENERATION

A New Life from God. An Inward Working in the Soul.
ITS NECESSITY (John 3:7; Galatians 6:15; Ephesians 2:2)

ITS NATURE (John 3:5; II Corinthians 5:17; Ephesians 2:10; 4:24)

ITS AGENT (John 3:8; 6:63; II Corinthians 3:6; Titus 3:5)

ITS INSTRUMENT (I Peter 1:23; James 1:18; John 5:24)

ITS MEANS (I John 5:1; Galatians 3:26; John 1:12-13)

ITS FRUITS (I John 3:9; Romans 6:22; I John 3:10)

ITS MANIFESTATION (I John 5:1-2; 3:16)

—500 *Bible Subjects*

REST

There are at least three words translated "rest" in the New Testament.

I. ANAPAUSIS — "an up rest," as in Matthew 11:28
II. KATAPAUSIS — "A down rest," as in Hebrews 4:4
III. SABBATISMOS — "a Sabbath rest," as in Hebrews 4:9
IV. KINDS OF REST

A. Rest for the Sinner (Matthew 11:28) — At the Cross

B. Rest for the Saint (Matthew 11:29) — In Subjection

C. Rest in the Lord (Psalm 36:7) — In Confidence

D. Rest with the Lord (II Thessalonians 1:7) — In Glory

E. Rest that Remains (Hebrews 4:9) — Eternal

—500 *Bible Subjects*

SYMBOLS OF THE WORD

A MIRROR to show us ourselves (James 1:23)

A HAMMER to break the bill (Jeremiah 23:29)

A FIRE to melt the heart (Jeremiah 23:29)

A SWORD to pierce the conscience (Hebrews 4:12)

A SEED to quicken the soul (I Peter 1:23)
A LAVER to cleanse the way (Ephesians 5:26)
A LIGHT to shew the path (Psalm 119:105)
—*500 Bible Subjects*

TEMPTATION

I. YOU CAN'T AVOID IT
  A. But you can avoid experiences that bring it on
II. HOW SHOULD YOU MEET IT?
  A. Remember That Satan is Behind It All
    1. He knows how to get us
      a. Through our strong point
      b. Through our weak point
  B. Every time we give in, it means more trouble next time
III. HOW TO MEET TEMPTATION
  A. Scripture (I Corinthians 10:13)
  B. Flee it (like Joseph)
  C. Avoid it
  D. Stand in faith (Like Jesus did)
  E. Don't entertain it
  F. Pick the right company
  G. Remember Jesus is praying for you
III. SUMMARY — HOW TO REMEMBER THESE POINTS
  A. Promise
  B. Provision
  C. Power
  D. Prayer
V. WHAT TO DO IF YOU FAIL
  A. Confess Your Sin and Try Again
                                          —*500 Bible Subjects*

THE THREE SALVATIONS

But God who is rich in mercy, for his great love wherewith he loved us when we were dead in sins, hath quickened us together with Christ; by grace ye are saved (Ephesians 2:4-5). *Work out your own salvation with fear and trembling; for it is God that worketh in you both to will and to do of his own good pleasure* (Philippians 2:12, 13). *Now is our salvation nearer than when we believed* (Romans 13:11).

I. THERE IS A PAST, A PRESENT AND A FUTURE TENSE WHEN WE CONJUGATE THE WORD "SAVED." The believer has been saved, is being saved, and is to be saved.

    A. Salvation means deliverance — deliverance from some kind of danger or evil.

        1. In the first text it means deliverance from the *guilt* of *sin*.

        2. In the second from the *power* of *sin*.

        3. In the third from the *penalty* of *sin*.

    B. These three deliverances include pardon, sanctification and glorification.

        1. Pardon does not include sanctification, nor do these two include the third.

        2. Each blessing is distinct from the others.

    C. We are not to rest content with the first, as we are too apt to do.

    D. Do you want the second, for deliverance from the thrall, the bondage of sin?

II. LET US EXAMINE MORE CAREFULLY THESE THREE SALVATIONS.

    A. The Deliverance from Guilt.

        1. "There is no condemnation to them that are in Christ Jesus." To the penitent one Jesus said, "Thy sins be forgiven thee." In that sense, O child of God, thou hast already been saved.

        2. But Jesus added, "Go, and sin no more."

And this brings us to the thought in the second text, namely,

B. Deliverance from the Power of Sin.

C. And What of the Hereafter?
  1. "It doth not yet appear."
  2. "We shall be like him."
  3. "He shall change these vile bodies."
  4. "When he shall appear a second time without sin unto salvation."

III. THERE IS TO BE A FINAL AND GLORIOUS DELIVERANCE FROM THE POWER OF DEATH AND THE GRAVE, AND THIS DELIVERANCE, this salvation, "is nearer than when we first believed."

—*Revival Sermons in Outline*
F. B. MEYER

SCRIPTURE INDEX

TITLE INDEX